Doone Raynham

The
GRIFFON
BRUXELLOIS

Second Edition

Acknowledgements

I would like to thank Mrs Mollie Grocolt, Mrs Gunn-Ell Sehlstedt, Mr and Mrs Christer Jernhake, Mr Richard A Ball, Mrs Priscilla Wells and Mr Jan den Otter.

I am much indebted to them for their kind contribution of articles for the overseas chapter. My thanks also to Mrs Maureen Higgins for her specialised knowledge of the black Griffon Bruxellois. My thanks to The Kennel Club for permission to reproduce the Breed Standard. I should also like to thank all the professional photographers, including Mr Fall and Mrs Burrows, who have been so kind. I would like to acknowledge the help and encouragement of friends and their many personal photographs. Finally, my thanks go to my son-in-law Paul Lees who deciphered the manuscript and my daughter Christina Lees ABIPP who so patiently photographed my own dogs, to my great appreciation.

Front Cover: Ch Dorelove Jimmy Mac, owned and bred by Mr and Mrs N Swan.

DEDICATION

To my family and all the many friends Dick and I have made in the company of the Griffon Bruxellois

KINGDOM

Contents

History of the Griffon Bruxellois

The Griffon Bruxellois has been said to be a *parvenu* – a 19th century hotch-potch of several breeds that, more by luck than judgement, resulted in the dog we have today. Its origin is something of a mystery because if, as has been suggested by some exponents, the Griffon did not have any identity before the 19th century, it is strange that small dogs greatly resembling the Griffon Bruxellois were featured by artists long before that time. A painting by the artist Jan van Eyck dated 1434 can be seen in the National Gallery. Entitled *The Marriage of Arnolfini and Giovanna Cenani*, it depicts a Griffon-type dog. During the 16th century Jacope de Empolin also painted Griffon-type dogs, albeit Griffons in need of stripping! In 1870 Renoir painted *La Baigneuse au Griffon* (The Bather with a Griffon). For a painting to have Griffon in its title might make one suppose the breed was already quite well known.

An etching of *Bibi and Coquette*, origin unknown.

Whatever its antecedents, whether back to the 15th century or within the last century, it is generally accepted that the breed is native to Belgium, and the first Griffon Bruxellois was imported from there into England.

From the little information available regarding early Griffons in Europe it would seem that, although some of the continental Royal Families kept Griffons as pets, they were much more likely to be found on the waterfronts and in the stables, particularly in the Brussels area of Belgium, where the cabbies kept them as ratting dogs. They used to ride on their masters' *fiacres* and became well-known for their monkey faces and pert expressions, which endeared them to passers-by.

During the 1880s the first Breed Standard was drawn up and in 1883 the first breed classes were classified at dog shows in Belgium. One of the early Belgian show dogs was a female called Miss, owned by a hackney coachman in La Place Royale; she produced a celebrated stud dog known as Champion Fox. Champion Fox was mated to a small Yorkshire Terrier and produced another well-known dog called Petit Fox. A stud dog called Petit Waterloo was mated to a female Pug and produced a dog known as Tom who sired a number of winners and is said to be a distant ancestor of many modern dogs.

There were some strange stories of early faking and potential owners were warned to be on their guard against the colour of their Griffon washing out once they had made a purchase. Perhaps the strangest story is one of a street trader in the Bois de Boulogne whose little Griffon was doing tricks, to the amusement of people strolling in the *Bois*. When a lady wanted to buy the little dog, she was persuaded by the owner to buy instead an even smaller one he had in his pocket. On arriving home with her new acquisition, the lady took the little dog from her muff and put it down on the floor, where apparently the dog took a quick look around and shinned up a curtain rail. Eventually it was retrieved by a footman and the lady was horrified to find her little dog was a rat sewn up in a Griffon skin!

In about 1894 Queen Astrid of the Belgians, who was interested in several breeds of dog, became attracted to the Griffon Bruxellois and started to breed these dogs and improve their quality. As a result of such royal interest the Griffon in Belgium became very fashionable.

Shortly after the First World War there were about 5000 female Griffons in Belgium, most them in the Brussels area. It is incredible that, after such popularity, there are not so many in the whole of Belgium today.

Luckily the story in Britain is very different. The earliest importations were around 1880 and registered ones occurred in 1894, when Mrs Kingscote, Miss Adela Gordon, Mrs Frank Pearce and Mr Fletcher (a London dog-dealer) all imported Griffons Bruxellois. Shortly afterwards Lady Handley Spicer also imported some dogs. The first Griffons to achieve championship honours in Britain were Bruno, bred in Belgium by Monsieur Tielemans in 1895 and owned

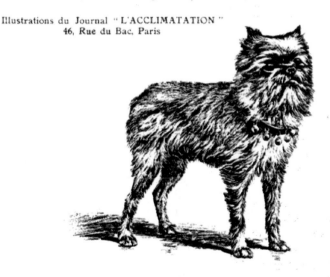

Illustrations du Journal " L'ACCLIMATATION "
46, Rue du Bac, Paris

Race GRIFFON BRUXELLOIS
Chien de Dame, 1er Prix, à Paris.

An early illustration of a Griffon Bruxellois.

in England by Miss Wimbush, followed by Mousequetaire Rouge and litter sister Marquerite Rouge, born 1899, bred and owned by Mrs Moseley.

During a visit to Longleat in 1975 I discovered two early Griffon graves: of Shrimp who died in 1907 and Peter who died in 1919. Both dogs were pets of the fifth Marchioness of Bath and buried in the Bath family pet cemetery along with other dogs and birds. Unfortunately, the inscriptions on the Griffon graves are now almost obliterated but may still be of interest to Griffon owners visiting the famous house and Safari Park.

GRIFFON BRUXELLES "MARQUIS DE CARABAS" COUNT DE BYLANDT owner

A Griffon Bruxellois owned by the Count de Bylandt.

During the late 19th century there was considerable discussion on how the Griffon Bruxellois evolved. In 1898 Count de Bylandt, described by the 'Dog Owners Supplement' to *The Bazaar* as the most knowledgeable authority on the Griffon, said the breed was a cross between the King Charles Spaniel and the Affenpinscher. The Count further expanded his theory to include in the cross an infusion of the Toy Bulldog and the Pug. These theories were disputed by Mr Rawdon Lee, an Englishman who said the Griffon originated in Britain and was a cross between the Irish Terrier and the Yorkshire Terrier. There were others who claimed that the North Country Red Navvy Terrier, a little dog bred by miners, was also used in the original Griffon breeding. It was said that the miners took these dogs to work for company, carrying them in their large pockets.

It is interesting to note that the German Wirehaired Pinscher slightly resembles the Irish Terrier, which in turn has a claim on Griffon ancestry. However, if the Pinscher is part of the ancestry, it would have to be the miniature variety, and this theory would only stand up if indeed the Griffon is of relatively modern origin. The Belgians claim there have been Griffons of varying types in Brussels since time immemorial and, considering the large numbers that were kept, this fact is not easy to dispute.

In 1897 the Griffon Bruxellois Club was formed to look after the welfare of Griffons and in 1899 The Kennel Club gave Griffons varietal ranking and they were no longer to be known as a foreign dog. Up until that date Griffons could only be registered in the 'Foreign Section' of *The Kennel Club Stud Book*. In 1902 the Brussels Griffon Club of London was formed and was said to be more vigorous than the parent club; a little later a club was formed to care for Griffons of *any other colour than red*. That club did not last very long and the Brussels Griffon Club of London was also terminated. Thus only the Griffon Bruxellois Club survived the First World War to look after Griffons of all colours.

One of the best-known and most successful kennels at the beginning of the 20th century was that of Lady Handley Spicer of the Copthorne affix, who made up 14 champions in the first 12 years of the century. Miss Hall of the Park Place kennel, the Misses Plunket of Castlehaven and Mrs Parker Rhodes of the Partridge Hill kennel were amongst many well-known exhibitors. Many of the early British Griffon breeders lived in London and the Home Counties. The Hon Mrs Ionides of Orleans House, Twickenham, kept a kennel of 30 breeding bitches, all within the confines of her home, where she studied to improve the breed. It is perhaps an insight into the lady to learn that puppies played together in the ballroom!

The first Griffon classes to be scheduled and judged separately in Britain took place in 1898 at the Ladies Kennel Club Association Show. This was probably due to the interest of Lady Handley Spicer, who was on the committee of that association.

When Griffons were first exhibited there were many more black-and-tans than there are today. It has even been suggested that this was the original colour, but again it is a disjointed theory. However, it is interesting to note that in 1911 *The Illustrated Kennel News* reported that a feature of the Ladies Kennel Association Members Show was the large number of black-and-tan Griffons in an entry of 47

dogs. Perhaps the most illuminating quote on colour was made in 1913 by Lady Handley Spicer, who said at that time that she 'considered Black and Tan Griffons to be *bona fide* specimens of the breed because their origin went so far back in time'.

Lady Handley Spicer, who held Griffons with such affectionate regard and was a much respected authority on the breed, died in 1963 aged 91.

During the years before the First World War Challenge Certificates (CCs) were awarded for both rough and smooth Griffons, which indicates the recognition of a variety of types within the breed at that time.

A head study of a Griffon Bruxellois, dated 1921.

Introducing the Griffon

The Griffon Bruxellois has been described as a small cobby dog, approximately 35cm (14in) to point of shoulder, with a rounded head, large eyes and an upturned jaw. The nose should be well laid back with open nostrils and these features combine to give the dogs their endearing, monkey-like expression. The body should be short with well sprung ribs, a broad chest, level top line, standing four square on solid legs, giving the impression of measuring the same amount from shoulder to croup (point of tail) as shoulders to the ground.

The colours are red, black or black-and-tan. There is also the Griffon Belge whose coat is a mixture of black and red sometimes incorrectly referred to as a brindle (a genuine brindle is a patterned marking of red and black in each hair). The latter type is recognised in the United States and on the Continent but it is not accepted in Britain. At one time the United States did not recognise the black smooth Griffon on the grounds that in type it was too similar to the Pug, but this rule has since been rescinded and the black smooth is now accepted. This is also the case in most Continental countries.

The Griffon is a very intelligent, sturdy breed of Toy Dog and not prone to many ills. Griffons like to be kept warm but, other than that, do not require any special pampering and normally live for 12 to 15 years and even beyond, during which time they are capable of giving their owners much pleasure and companionship. It is a fact that pet owners, once they have owned a Griffon Bruxellois, rarely change to a different breed when the time comes to replace their pets.

'I see no signal!'

'What *are* you doing?' A surprised five-month-old red pup is accosted by some smaller, hungry friends.

Griffons are bred with either rough or smooth coats. *Bruxellois* actually means *from Brussels*, but in breed terms it means a rough-coated dog. *Petit Brabançon* refers to the smooth-coated variety of Griffon. Collectively they are known as *Griffons Bruxellois*. For simplicity I will refer to them as *rough* or *smooth* throughout the book. When talking about the breed, it is necessary to add *Bruxellois* to avoid confusion with the Petit Basset Griffon Vendéen, a totally different breed of dog.

The red rough or, as some might term it, russet-coated Griffon is considered the most popular variety, but now the red smooth is catching up fast in the popularity stakes. Many more of this type can be seen in the show ring today. The Breed Standard as laid down by The Kennel Club states: *The colour of a red rough dog should be a clear red.* However the shade varies considerably from a sandy wheaten shade to a deep chestnut. The colour probably does not matter too much to the pet owner; some prefer the pale colour to the predetermined shade of red. The red smooth Petit Brabançon should be a bright rich red: something resembling a horse-chestnut might describe the colour most desired.

There is an infrequently-mentioned colour condition with red rough Griffons whereby the colour does not extend the entire length of each hair. The colour often fades when the coat ages and needs stripping out. In the very deep coloured reds the colour reaches down to the roots of the hair, but in dogs where the colour does extend to the full length of the hair there may also be a general lack of black pigmentation. In other words, the black circular markings around the eyes can be missing, the eyes can be lighter than one likes to see and the toenails brownish rather than the required black. This colour variation is not confined to Griffons: the ruby Cavalier King Charles, also a very strong colour, can have a problem with its pigment. However, this is of no interest to the pet owner, being purely a matter of coat perfection for the exhibitor.

The black rough Griffon is relatively easy to obtain now that more breeders specialise in the colour. The black smooth Petit Brabançon is very rare indeed and seldom seen even in the show ring.

There are very few smooth or rough black-and-tan Griffons, despite renewed interest during the 1950s in a colour that was popular much earlier. Numbers probably dwindled with the onset of the Second World War, when so much dog

Ch Dorelove Maggi May at four months playing in the sand.

breeding was curtailed or ceased altogether. Today black-and-tans are difficult to breed because of sheer lack of numbers.

The rough Griffon does not really moult and needs to be stripped once or twice a year. The thought of stripping can be a little daunting, but it is not too difficult. There is the added bonus that you do not have to vacuum hair off your carpets or have hair-covered cushions. However, it must also be said that, provided the owners keep a smooth dog well brushed, they should have very little trouble with loose hair. The smooth-coated Griffon does not moult like a Terrier or Dalmatian. One point of interest to some prospective owners is that Griffons do not usually affect children who suffer from asthma.

The temperament of the vast majority of Griffons is excellent; they are friendly, obedient companions, interested in everything you do and always anxious to help. I do not think there is any great difference in temperament between the rough and smooth dogs. It is often said that the smooth dogs are more outgoing and lively, the rough more restrained in character, but it is largely a matter of opinion and perhaps upbringing. The over-riding decision is probably whether you want a smooth or a bearded face on your Griffon.

The choice of sex for a pet in a small breed of dog does not really matter. Some potential owners would never consider buying a female because of their seasons, whilst others feel that bitches are more faithful and, as someone once remarked to me, they do not want to stop at every lamppost! Personally I would not agree that male dogs are less faithful. They can be just as affectionate as females and, if properly trained, do not stop at all when out for a walk unless let off the lead in a safe area.

A female Griffon does have to be watched when she is in season, normally for about three weeks every six months or so. The last two weeks of a season is the period when you have to be particularly careful that your female does not meet up with male dogs. Preparations can be bought nowadays to make a female of less interest to males, which is a great advantage to the owner. There are also types of birth control pills, or the bitch can be spayed if you do not intend to breed from her. A veterinary surgeon will always advise owners about this. Female Griffons are so clean that it is not always noticeable when they are in season, and some females have colourless seasons, which can add to the difficulty of diagnosis.

The Griffon makes an excellent house dog. Its acute hearing will tell you when anybody is approaching your domain long before you are aware of visitors yourself. When I lived on a farm I could differentiate the type of bark warning that someone was in the farmyard, that someone was at the garden gate, or that a cow was out – the latter situation causing uproarious barking!

Some friends of ours have a Griffon who, if he gets the chance, posts the letters and papers back through the flap of the letter box should the postman or paper boy not be quick enough in getting the letter box flap down. The owner says the dog is protecting his home and considers items through the letter box an invasion of his privacy. Another dog, a retired champion of mine, barks *sotto voce* at the morning papers until her owner comes to pick them up. My own dogs conveniently tell me if the telephone is ringing when I am in the garden and cannot hear the bell. Best of all perhaps are the dogs like Young Claude, whose acute hearing late one night foiled an intruder; his barking alerted his owners.

Having decided on sex, coat and colour, the next step to obtaining your Griffon is to look at the advertisements in the dog papers such as *Dog World* and *Our Dogs,* which can be ordered from your newsagent. The local papers in your particular district can also be tried, but may not prove very rewarding, because Griffons are not often advertised for sale in them.

A letter or telephone call to The Kennel Club in London will provide any prospective purchaser with names and addresses of breeders in your area. Armed with your list, you have taken the first step toward the great moment of acquiring your first Griffon Bruxellois.

Family friends – not all Griffons are 'specist'!

Buying a Griffon

Buying a puppy

Most Griffon breeders are commendably protective of their puppies. Prospective owners who have located or heard of an expected litter will have to satisfy the breeder of their genuine interest and capability of caring for puppies. Good dog breeders are very helpful, able to suit the prospective owner to a puppy and willing to keep in touch and give help and advice if it is needed.

As a guide, the 1997 price for a well reared puppy would be in the region of £300, the price varying according to its breeding and show potential. The ever-escalating cost of raising, registering and inoculating a puppy must continue to have an effect on the valuation of a puppy in the next century, making all breeds of dog more expensive, but can one relate in monetary terms the value of many years of companionship?

When buying a puppy the prospective owner should inquire whether the puppy has been wormed and, if it is old enough, inoculated. If the puppy has not been wormed, the new owner would be advised to ask the breeder to undertake this necessary task well before the puppy goes to its new home, thus avoiding any upset to the puppy's routine. However, it is fairly safe to say that worming will have been done as a matter of routine by the breeder.

I like to give a repeat worming at five months old or so, which in my kennel is usually a few weeks before I start showing a puppy. It is always a good idea to make sure that your pet puppy is quite clear of worms before it becomes adult, and thereafter your dog must be treated at least once a year. I must stress that, in any worming I do, I err on the side of a slightly smaller dose than that prescribed because, once you have given the medicine, you cannot call it back!

The choice of inoculations is wide today, some starting at eight weeks and others the more usual twelve and fourteen weeks. If your puppy is already inoculated, the breeder will provide you with a certificate of inoculation: if not, your veterinary surgeon will advise when the puppy should be inoculated. Opinions vary, the most usual age being twelve weeks, with a booster at six to twelve months, depending on the particular vaccine used on the puppy. Inoculations are given to puppies for the prevention of distemper, hepatitis, leptospirosis and parvovirus.

It is important to maintain the same type of diet in the new home as that given to the puppy by the breeder. An efficient breeder will provide a diet sheet, which should be adhered to if tummy upsets are to be avoided and the puppy is to thrive in its new environment.

You will be given a registration and pedigree certificate. The certificate is filled in by both breeder and owner and then sent to The Kennel Club for the transfer to be effected. The pedigree usually goes back through five generations; it reads from left to right and champions are normally entered in red ink.

Some breeders will provide the new owner with a small collar and lead

PEDIGREE CERTIFICATE OF ....

BREED .. *Griffon Bruxellois*

COLOUR and Markings .. *Red Rough.*

BREEDER .. *Ann Fenn*   Kennel Club Registration No. ....   Date of Registration ....

OWNER ....

DATE OF BIRTH .. *22.09.84* ex. *Dog.*   ADDRESS ....

KENNEL NAME .. *Ch. Starbeck Crystal Rainbow*

KENNEL CLUB STUD BOOK No. ....   SIGNED ....   DATE ....

PARENTS	GRAND-PARENTS	GREAT GRAND-PARENTS	GREAT GREAT GRAND-PARENTS
SIRE Ch Starbeck Citation	Ch Starbeck Chindit	Ch/Am.Ch. Starbeck Chinrullah	Rainbow Won
		Ch Starbeck Columbine	12 Groups, 3 B.I.S. All Breeds
	Ch Starbeck Cristabelle	Rowell Golddigger	3 Reserve B.I.S. All-Breeds
		Ch Starbeck Cristaminta	2 B.I.S. GBC. CH. 2 Group & at Crufts
DAM Starbeck Cristallina	Starbeck Cracaval	Ch Starbeck Fusilier	Top Griffon 1986, '87 & '88.
		Ch Starbeck Chingle Bell	x
	Starbeck Celestial Jewel	Ch/Am. Ch. Starbeck Chinrullah	x
		Starbeck Fire Angel	x

(Copyright) OUR DOGS, Manchester

SIGNED *A.M. Fenn*   DATE ....

The pedigree certificate of Ch Starbeck Crystal Rainbow – a red entry indicates a champion.

because such small sizes are not readily available in local pet shops. I have always given new owners a little narrow collar and separate matching lead. Unfortunately, these are unobtainable at the moment and I now keep a little stock of very small rolled leather collars and matching nylon leads. Even when adult the Griffon does not need anything heavier than that, although the little rolled collar may need to be replaced with a larger size as the puppy gets older. A collar should not be too tight around the puppy's neck but the puppy should not be able to pull the collar over its head. By law a dog has to have an identity disc and I find that cat size discs are the most suitable for Griffons; they are not too heavy and do not dangle down far enough to irritate the dog.

The puppy arriving in its new home requires love and attention to help it settle in: it should be shown its own basket or cardboard box, which should be lined with a nice woolly blanket, and generally made to feel welcome. Do not smother the puppy with attention but be considerate of its needs, remembering that puppies must have plenty of sleep as well as plenty of affection. Please also consider how strange it is for the young puppy, suddenly bereft of its dam and siblings. Griffon puppies are very adaptable and usually settle within 48 hours by taking over and behaving as though they have been with you for ever.

Many puppies raised indoors are trained to relieve themselves on newspaper, so spread some paper about wherever your puppy's basket or box is situated. When I am raising a litter and the puppies are old enough to leave the confinement of an indoor pen, I spread newspaper around the garden door and, in the summer when it is warm enough for the door to be kept open, the puppies play in the garden and pop back dutifully to relieve themselves on the paper! All this eventually resolves itself naturally and the puppies are clean at a very early age. When you have one new puppy, probably already partly trained, you must take the puppy out into the garden yourself – it is unkind to expect a young puppy to go out into a strange garden by itself and perform. When your puppy obliges, make a fuss of it and return indoors. Puppies soon learn to understand what is expected of them and wish to please. Never chastise a puppy for the occasional mishap – just cheerfully take the puppy out a little more often. If you have to leave your pet, even when it is adult, for a considerable period during the day, thoughtful provision of a little newspaper on the floor can prevent distress for a little dog who can wait no longer.

A puppy has to learn who its master or mistress is, or both master *and* mistress if there are several people in the household. Puppies need to feel safe and will attach themselves to one or two people. The owners should feed the puppy, play with it and teach it to come when called.

From the diet sheet supplied by the breeder you will see that, from weaning, puppies are fed three to four times a day, plus two drinks of milk, and always have fresh water freely available. Some people feed them a cereal breakfast and supper with two meat meals during the day. Farleys rusks are excellent food value and many other baby cereals are equally suitable for puppies. Some dog breeders have their own special mixture of a variety of baby foods.

It is virtually impossible to overfeed a puppy but never leave food down once the puppy has had enough; pick up the bowl and provide fresh food at the next meal – then you will know how much a puppy will eat at each meal. Of course as the puppy grows the size of each meal has to be increased. You will quite often find that a puppy will indicate when you can drop from four to three meals and, by the time the puppy is around six months or so, to two meals a day. Some adult dogs need two meals a day, but one meal is normally sufficient. Generally speaking, the owner has to be guided by the condition of the dog and natural common sense.

Apart from fresh meat and poultry to mix with biscuits there is a simply staggering number of alternatives in hard complete foods and semi-soft ones. They all now have extremely high vitamin content plus the other necessities which go to make up a complete diet.

The choice of tinned foods, complete or to use with a mixer, is also vast. As well as tinned, there are the foiled varieties of complete foods which, although a little more expensive, are very popular.

Experts tell us that a dog does not need to have a varied diet and one should keep to a routine method of feeding. However, the manufacturers continue to dazzle us with a massive array of food for show dogs, working dogs, breeding dogs and pet dogs. I suspect they think that, considering our own mixed diet, we like to offer our dogs a varied diet too. My own puppies sometimes prefer a certain brand of tinned food to the normally-accepted basic diet of raw minced beef that dog breeders, including myself, have used for many years to raise puppies. This can also be tried for dogs on a single complete diet who go off their food. A change, if only momentarily, to something

Ch Mahnyar Dragonfly and family.

It's not easy to spot a future champion in a litter; Ch Fromebank Eastend Lad. Photo: Lionel Young

else gets them back to eating and then, quite often, happily back to their original diet.

Puppies should have hard biscuits to try their teeth on. These may have to be broken up a little for the very young puppy. They can also have a rounded marrow bone with no small pieces adhering to it. Never give any dog chicken bones or similar types of bone.

I have only mentioned fresh meat in passing. The most often used is minced beef, which can be served raw or cooked, depending how the dog likes it; some dogs do not like raw meat. Hearts, ox cheek or mutton breasts are all good food value. The latter are best cooked in the oven until the fat is crisp and then well drained. Chicken is a great favourite, and rabbit too if you can obtain it. Liver can be fed in careful moderation, perhaps a little every 10 days or so: too much causes tummy trouble. Liver should never be fed to a young puppy. Tripe (either raw or cooked) is often used, and should be either minced or cut very fine. To vary the diet, puppies and adults often like cheese, scrambled or boiled eggs or a little piece of bacon. Some dogs also enjoy fruit, such as orange, apple or grapes. Some dogs like fish, which is very good for them, but great care has to be taken to avoid the bones in most fish.

There are many different brands of tinned dog food, all nationally advertised and seen on television. They can be served straight from the tin or mixed with biscuit meal.

In recent years dog food manufacturers have brought out several types of red soft complete foods, looking like either mince or meat in a cube form. It is to be remembered that, with any brand of complete food, the dog will need to drink much more water than when fed on fresh meat.

Whether you add any vitamin supplement to your dog's diet depends entirely on what you are giving it – many biscuit meals and all complete foods have all the necessary vitamins in them. However, if the dog is eating less than the prescribed amount for its size and age, a supplement might be advisable. Again many additives from which you can choose are widely advertised in the dog press; alternatively, veterinary advice can be sought.

Griffon Bruxellois puppies do not need any exercise; the garden is quite sufficient while they are young and it is not wise to exercise a puppy until after it is six months old. A short walk does not matter particularly if you require the company your puppy provides; I am thinking about the diehards who assume that, if they have a puppy, it must be walked. More damage can be done to a puppy through too much exercise than too little. Young bones need time to grow and strengthen. When a puppy is about nine months old, owners will find that their pet is quite accommodating. If you like long walks the dog will enjoy them too, but if you do not they will be equally happy so long as they are with you.

Nine-week-old black-and-tans. Photo: Christina Lees

Buying an older dog

Some people may not wish to buy a puppy, preferring an older dog, already trained, who can be an instant companion and go for walks right away.

It is sometimes possible to obtain an adult dog either by buying or on a permanent loan from a Griffon breeder. Such a breeder would have to be completely happy about where the dog is going, and that the prospective owner will give the dog as much, or even more, love and attention than it has already enjoyed. Some pet owners may think it is a little unkind for a breeder to part with an adult dog. However, Griffon breeders are very caring people: that is what allows them to let certain adult dogs go into pet homes to enjoy all the extra fuss and attention of a smaller household, stoically covering up their own personal loss (which can last a long time) for the dog's wellbeing, knowing that it is happily settled as a pet.

Jack and Harry: two Cleevecloud rascals.

A beautiful litter of red smooth puppies.

Everyday Care of the Griffon

A place of its own

Your dog needs a basket or box of its own in a corner of the kitchen or living room. Even if the dog is allowed to sleep on the owner's bed, it does need somewhere to take its possessions that is its own territory.

The majority of Griffon breeders do not keep their dogs in outside kennels, most having them as pets who live in the house or in indoor kennels. The dogs sometimes have a room of their own within the home. Some breeders

A carrying box: useful for transport, but too small for a bed.

have indoor tiered box kennels in which the dogs can be placed for individual feeding or when there are guests in the house who may not appreciate doggy overtures. Such boxes are a great convenience and some dogs like to have their own particular 'room' to sleep in. No dog, however, should be expected to spend long periods in this type of box.

Feeding

Young adults sometimes need two meals a day: their stomachs are small and they cannot always cope with too much food at one time. The amount of food given at a single meal should balance out in favour of whatever meat or chicken is offered. Griffons do need a certain amount of carbohydrate but not an excess of it. On average a Griffon will eat 85–140g (3–6oz) of meat a day. Much depends on the size of the dog.

The suggestion of not leaving food on the floor for a puppy to return to if and when it feels like it does not apply to the adult dog. Some adults do not eat their food all at once, others prefer to eat at night, and some will not eat at all if their owner is in the room. The most suitable type of feeding bowl is a round plastic or metal container, about 12.5cm (5in) in circumference which can easily be washed out separately under the tap.

Vitamins

Vitamins and minerals are necessary to a dog's well-being, but owners should be aware that some additives such as the A and D groups can be harmful if over-indulged. All complete foods and many cereal mixes already have minerals added to them. If you are in any doubt, consult your breeder or vet.

Water bowls

Given the choice between a large and a small drinking bowl, some Griffons will choose the smaller to avoid getting their whiskers wet in a large expanse of water. Others will test the depth of water in a large bowl with their paw, which often looks as though they are intending to tip the bowl over. The smaller bowl is preferable, but do ensure that adequate water is always available.

Flowers

I have found when arranging flowers or coping with house-plants that it is necessary to be very careful not to drop cut-off pieces of stalk. Some plants and flowers are poisonous to dogs. For instance, a Griffon who runs off with a small piece of daffodil stalk will be very sick after just a little chew.

Travel sickness

Puppies can be very sick on their first journey to a new home because of the strangeness of the situation and the necessity of becoming accustomed to a new family without the support of dam, siblings and breeder. It usually resolves itself happily as soon as the puppy is settled in its new home.

Persistent sickness in an adult dog who travels frequently is very distressing for the dog and a worry for the owner. Most small dogs travel better on somebody's lap rather than in a travelling box or cage, but this is impossible if the dog is likely to be sick over you! The remedy I find most effective is a half a tablet of SeaLegs

On average, a Griffon eats 85–140g of meat a day.

(a human travel sickness tablet) given the evening before the journey. Travel sickness tablets specially prepared for dogs can be obtained from pet shops and trade counters at Championship Shows.

Bathing

Dogs should be bathed whenever they need it.

Dogs and puppies should be bathed whenever they happen to need it. There is nothing worse than a dog that has rolled in something totally unsavoury endeavouring to curl up on your lap!

There are plenty of different brands of dog shampoo for ordinary use and insecticidal shampoos for dogs with itchy coats resulting from dandruff or mites picked up from the grass. In cases of extreme irritation consult your vet.

When I bath a dog I wash the face and ears with a Baby Shampoo to avoid any possibility of hurting the dog's eyes. The rest of the body I wash with a herbal shampoo and rinse well with clean water. If the dog has any sort of back irritation I use a combined insecticidal and dandruff shampoo along the back, chest and legs, avoiding all the delicate parts. Dry with towels and, in winter, apply a little talc to the lower tummy. Some people use hair dryers, which is fine if the dog is accustomed to it, but some may object to this method.

Noses

A Griffon may occasionally develop a dry, cracked-looking nose. This can easily be remedied by the application of a little grease, such as butter, on the nose.

Grooming

The first essential is a work surface at which the owner can work comfortably sitting down. Old card tables make excellent grooming tables and are also useful for general handling and stripping. Take great care that your puppy does not fall off. Older dogs adjust quickly, but do not let them jump down from a height.

A dog will benefit from a good brushing, if not every day, at least two or three times a week. Brushing tones up the muscles as well as removing any dust or dandruff. A small-toothed comb run through the coat will take out any dead hair and help keep the dog's coat looking tidy for a longer period of time. A smooth Griffon really needs grooming every day to remove any loose hair and should then be finished off with a soft cloth or chamois leather.

In days gone by, stud grooms used to say that a good grooming was equivalent to a good feed. Our dogs would not appreciate such a statement, but it does signify the importance that was attached to the regular care of coat and skin.

Nails

A dog's nails need clipping or filing when you can hear the sound of them as the dog walks on a hard surface. The easiest way to keep nails in trim is to file them once a week, but not everybody remembers the chore, and it is not long before the nails need clipping first before rounding off with a file. When nails are clipped it is best done by taking off very small pieces at a time (not one large piece). If this is done back to the natural curve of the nail, not too much is taken and there is no danger of making the nail bleed.

Care of ears in an adult dog

Dogs' ears should be looked at now and again to make sure they are clean and smell sweet. It is helpful in the prevention of ear canker carefully to pull out the hair growing from the centre of the ear canal and to keep the hair short by trimming with scissors on other parts inside the ear, occasionally sprinkling lightly with ear canker powder afterwards. Red and swollen ears should be left alone and veterinary advice should be sought immediately.

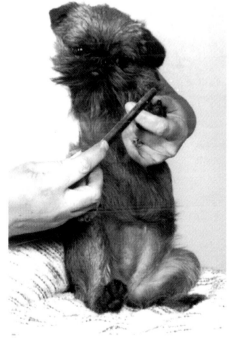

Anal glands in adult dogs

The anal glands are located under the tail, just below the anus. A dog who looks uncomfortable and is worrying its rear end or smells unpleasant may need its glands cleared. Failure to do so can lead to an abscess in that area.

Breeders usually check their own dogs regularly, while pet owners often

It is best to file your dog's nails once a week.

prefer their vet to do it for them. If you feel competent to do it yourself, place the dog on the grooming table. With your left hand, hold the tail upwards fairly tautly. With your right hand, feel the two glands and squeeze gently but firmly upwards to expel the fluid. Wipe with cotton wool or tissue and repeat until clean. Left-handed people will need to reverse the procedure.

House-training

It is very easy to house-train a puppy, particularly a Griffon who has been reared indoors. From early training with the breeder a puppy is half way to being clean by the time it arrives at its new home. During the day a puppy should be taken out when it wakes up, after feeding, when it has been playing, or when you intend to take it out with you in the car.

If there is a mishap where you particularly do not want one, try to pick the puppy up immediately and take it into the garden. Never smack a puppy for a mis-demeanour: a puppy has to learn by experience. Picking the puppy up quickly, taking it into the garden, and then praising it for doing what it should is the quickest method, and the puppy soon learns the accepted form of behaviour. Smacking a puppy for what it obviously does not understand can only lead to a cowering puppy with its outgoing personality permanently spoilt.

It is a good idea for dog owners to keep a special covered pail and shovel to keep the garden clean and fresh by cleaning up droppings every day.

Lead-training

Griffon puppies are not usually difficult to lead-train. There is always the odd one who is obstinate, but normally they understand quickly what is expected of them and co-operate without any trouble.

First, put a little collar on the puppy for a short time each day until the puppy becomes accustomed to it. Then start the training by taking the puppy out, prefer-ably somewhere quiet, on its collar and lead. The puppy may follow at once or it may pull back. If the puppy pulls back, get down to its level and call it to you. When it responds, make a fuss of it. Then stand up and try again, talking to and encouraging the puppy as you go along. All training should be of short duration so that the puppy does not become tired or bored with the procedure.

Exercise

As previously mentioned, Griffon puppies should not be exercised at all. However, if you happen to be going out in the car, a walk at your journey's end, such as a short run on the sea shore or over the moors, is a treat and great fun for the puppy. The adult Griffon will usually enjoy as many walks as its owner likes to take. Of course there is the odd lazy-bones who will vanish at the sight of a lead but the vast majority of dogs enjoy going out for walks if their owner is able to take them.

Cars

All owners should be aware of the very serious problems of dogs left in cars during hot weather. Your pet may be in the habit of travelling with you and being left in the car with a partly-opened window while you shop or visit. However, no dog should be left in a car even with open windows during the summer. Despite their voiceless pleas, dogs are safer at home, because heatstroke can affect a small dog like the Griffon Bruxellois within 10 to 15 minutes of being left in a car. Since the very hot summer of 1990 most of us, especially those travelling and showing dogs, have worried about the possibility of our dogs becoming victims of heat stroke. Bottles of water for drinking and to dampen towels, even ice cubes and packs, together with car shades, are used by exhibitors to protect their dogs both at shows and on the homeward journey.

At home, pets are better when kept where they can find shade in the garden or retreat indoors if they prefer. Dogs should never, on any account, be left in cars, even with the windows open, during warm weather.

Dogs in public areas

A minority of people wish to ban dogs from various public places, such as parks, pointing out the danger of children catching toxocarasis as a result of contact from the parasite *Toxocara canis*. The actual chance of a child catching the disease is minute indeed; perhaps it is more an excuse by the anti-dog people to push their point of view. The people who do not like dogs never mention the risk from cats.

However, there is a valid point in that it is most unpleasant to have a child fall in dog excreta while playing in a public park or, for that matter, for anybody to walk in excreta in the streets. It is therefore up to careful dog owners to take their dogs out into their own gardens for the dog to relieve itself prior to the enjoyed run in the park and never allow a dog to be a nuisance. As an alternative, and in case of 'accidents', they could carry plastic bags with them to pick up the faeces and dispose of them on their return home.

The Griffon in old age

The elderly Griffon may become a trifle deaf and rheumaticky or develop a little heart trouble but, even so, many go on to live to between 14 and 16 years; the oldest I have heard of is 17 years.

Holly, an elderly champion of mine, still had all her teeth at 14 years and her sight was excellent. She had a good appetite and her coat remained a rich red through regular stripping, although age won the day with regard to her legs and chest, which I used to trim with scissors to avoid the lengthy process on an older dog. In winter Holly would become rheumaticky in her front legs and had to be lifted on and off chairs but, when the ducks went diving through the water in the pond, she would rush out into the garden along with the other dogs, the most militant barker of all!

If your Griffon's teeth – or some of them – are missing, its food should be minced or chopped very finely. Some elderly dogs lose weight and they may need extra food. Exercise should be ruled out for any elderly dog that is at all rickety on its legs.

Stripping

It is always possible to take a puppy to a professional dog parlour to be clipped but it is rather more difficult to find an establishment that can hand-strip your Griffon competently. Some owners do not mind their pets being clipped. However, it is totally unacceptable if you have any thoughts of showing, since clipping spoils the texture and colour of the Griffon Bruxellois coat.

There are some breeders who will strip Griffons of their own breeding, while others

Three Cynjon beauties, all in need of stripping.

will take in any Griffon for stripping and general care. Others will advise you where you can have your dog properly stripped in your own area. It is certainly easier to find someone to strip your Griffon professionally for you than it was in the past. The alternative is to do it yourself and, once you have mastered the technique, you may find that this is the best solution for you. This is particularly true if you want to show your puppy, because you can keep the coat tidy by regular attention.

If you have not been in the habit of grooming your puppy or dog on the table, you must now be prepared to do so, since it is an absolute necessity for stripping. The dog must accept gradually the habit of standing, sitting and lying down on the table and the owner must take care that the dog does not leap into mid-air if it is distracted by anything. The table should be of suitable height to allow you to sit in comfort and firm enough for the dog to feel confident that it will support its weight.

The first experience of stripping is quite often with a puppy and the correct time to remove the coat is when it begins to look untidy and shaggy. The ease with which the process can be done depends on the type of coat. Some puppies have a softish puppy coat which looks very pretty but initially can be a little more difficult to take out. The short-haired, harsher-coated puppies are a much easier proposition. As far as the softer coat is concerned, the owner will find that a con-

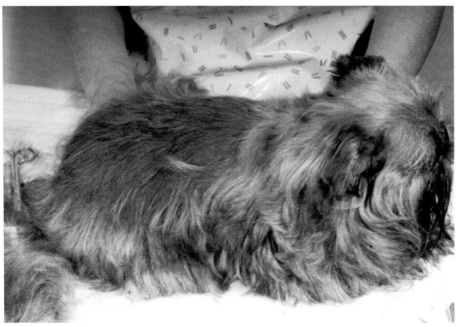

Delayed stripping – note new coat beneath.

siderable amount of hair has to be removed to encourage a strong growth of coarse hair. It may be necessary for the puppy to wear a little jacket if the weather is cold until the coat is through again because the undercoat may be sparse. The harsher type of puppy coat is very simple to strip out: just the guard hairs which stand away from the coat need to be taken out, leaving a perfectly tidy puppy.

In the adult Griffon, the harsher the coat, the shorter the length of the beard. A really soft-coated Griffon may have a long beard which looks charming, but it can be difficult to strip the coat of such a dog, which is tech-nically incorrect from the show point of view. However, not all soft-

These red rough puppies are ready for their first trim.

25

coated puppies will develop into soft-coated adults; many grow normal coats, and an ultra-harsh coat is the exception rather than the rule.

Preparing a coat for show requires perseverance. It is very difficult to have a Griffon coat looking good for the entire length of the show season. I used to write in my diary the date of stripping a dog, the time it took for the coat to come through and when the coat was ready for the dog to be shown again. This proved to have only a reminder value, since the exhibitor can be completely wrong. The weather in Britain is never predictable and some dogs are out of the show ring for many weeks from stripping to when there is enough coat to resume showing.

There are exhibitors who strip both top and undercoat at the same time. They say a dog stripped that way can be back in the show ring in six weeks because the coat grows so quickly. However, to me it seems rather like plucking a chicken, and what do you do with a naked dog during the hair growing time?

The top coat

The method of stripping I have adopted over the years is as follows:

- Place the dog on the table and make a fuss of it.
- Encourage it to lie down with its head away from you.
- Thoroughly brush and comb the coat.
- While one hand steadies the dog, take hold of a few hairs between thumb and forefinger of your other hand.
- Move them forwards, backwards and out.

Take a few hairs at a time and pull in the direction in which they are growing.

Every hair that you take out must be pulled out in the direction in which it grows. It sounds a violent procedure but, if the coat is ready, the hair will come out easily without any discomfort to the dog.

When stripping a dog, I start along the back, taking just a few hairs at a time in the manner described. Underneath the hair you are taking out you will find a soft undercoat, which you leave in until the new harsh coat begins to appear. Then the velvety coat is removed to leave the fresh grown top coat.

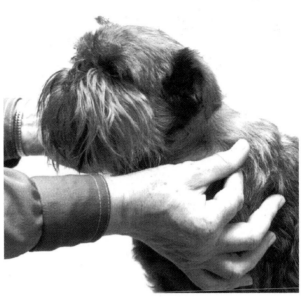

Ch Dozmare Della having her coat examined.

To return to the first task: after completely stripping the back, allow the dog to have a rest and start again later, or even the next day. You may find that your thumb and forefinger become sore if you are not used to stripping and try to do too much at a time. When I first started stripping dogs it would take me up to a week to complete the task. Now, without interruptions and with the dog's co-operation, I can do one in a day.

When the back has been stripped, the neck and head need attention, followed by chest and hindquarters. The area under the tail is fairly tender, so I strip where I can, carefully using trimming scissors in delicate places. The head also needs great care. Strip across the top and sides to eye level, where the beard begins, always allowing the beard itself to continue to grow. The hair on the ear flaps should be stripped off gently, leaving the hair as short as possible, particularly on the edges, to make them look as small as possible. I also trim off some of the hair in the ear: in the early days I stripped it all off, but here again it is a delicate area and to strip all the hair off can make the ear sore. The hair on the sides of the body and legs is very easy to strip. When doing the chest it is necessary to make sure that the hair is being stripped in the direction in which it grows, or it will be painful for the dog. Finally the tail needs doing and the lower parts of the tummy around the reproductive areas. Here again it is kinder to trim off the straggly long hair with scissors.

The feet should be examined and as much hair as possible stripped off. Then trim neatly to shape the rounded foot. The hair under the pads also needs tidying up with scissors and the nails should be kept short by cutting or filing.

The very harsh type of Griffon coat will last a whole season of showing

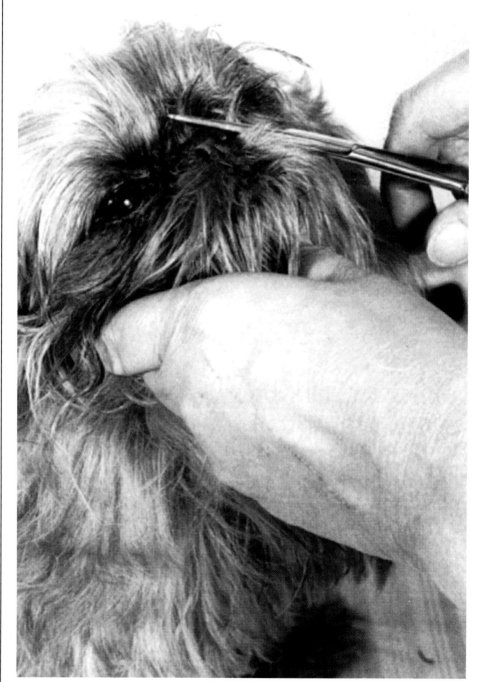

Trim the hair around the eyes into a fan.

without a complete strip; the coat is kept in good show condition by frequent tidying up sessions, never allowing the coat to become out of hand. After a winter stripping most Griffons need to wear a coat to keep warm until the new coat is well established.

Smooth Griffons do not require stripping, but the hair growing below the tail sometimes looks like a bustle and it improves the look of the dog if it is removed when the coat is loose. Depending on the coat quality, smooths also may need a jacket in very cold weather.

The undercoat

Ten or so years ago, when a Griffon's coat blew (grew out too quickly), an exhibit was withdrawn from the ring even if entered for further shows and did not return until the new coat had grown in sufficiently to please the judge. In those days, it was considered quite inappropriate to show a dog in what was termed by breeders as its *underclothes*.

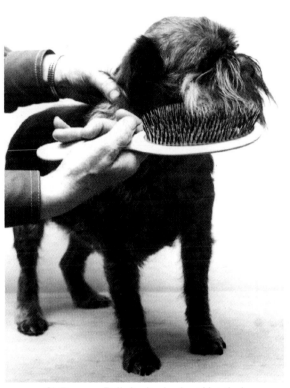

Nowadays, the *designer strip* seems here to stay. It is quite understandable that the exhibitor does not want to take an exhibit out of the ring because the coat has blown prematurely, especially if has been entered for several future shows. This type of strip is a very professional method and strictly not for the amateur.

Ch Dozmare Della having her beard brushed.

However, for the high-flyer it works wonders and the exhibit can go on winning major awards for an extended period.

For exhibits which have a rolling coat there is not the same problem. They can be shown for a whole season with just tidying up, every now and again. However, such coats are rare, seen only in very harsh-coated reds, blacks and black-and-tans.

The coat of the black-and-tan Griffon has a different make-up. It lies flat and close to the body and, when stripped, does not have the velvet pile of the red Griffon. The black-and-tan undercoat is so fine that it is part of the integral top coat, barely noticeable to the casual observer. If completely stripped the dog appears naked with just a minuscule covering of hair.

Breeding and Raising Puppies

The first black-and-tan puppies bred by the author.

The decision to breed a litter should not be taken lightly. Griffons are not easy to breed and experience with other breeds of small dogs is an advantage before you embark on Griffons. Many well-known enthusiasts can tell you of early failures and even current ones in their efforts to breed litters successfully. However, although several things can go wrong for the unsuspecting dog breeder, when all is well it is a heart-warming moment to watch your Griffon happily nursing her new-born puppies.

The season

Female Griffons usually come into season twice a year. A young bitch usually has her first season between six and nine months old but should not be bred from until she is fully mature at her second or preferably third season. Some young females are not psychologically ready for puppies.

From beginning to end a season lasts about three weeks. During the first week the vulva becomes much enlarged and by the second week there should be a coloured discharge. When this discharge turns colourless is regarded as the most reliable time for a female Griffon to conceive. The majority of breeders mate their females about the 10th or 12th day from the onset of the season but some females need to be mated either earlier or much later according to their particular cycle.

If you mate your Griffon to a selected dog, there will be at least a further week during which your bitch might accept the attention of another dog. It is therefore essential that she is kept away from all other males until you are certain she is out of season.

A Griffon puppy is a very small handful.

Choosing a stud

When you are choosing a stud dog to mate with your Griffon, it is advisable to select one of similar background and breeding to your bitch. You can tell this by studying the affixes on her pedigree. A permutation of line breeding, such as maternal grandfather to granddaughter, uncle to niece or cousin to cousin, can be very successful.

Direct inbreeding, such as mother to son and brother to sister, is not recommended unless undertaken by a very experienced breeder for a specific reason. This does not mean that, should an unplanned mating of this sort happen in your own ménage, you should rush to your veterinary surgeon for an injection to terminate the pregnancy; you could still have a nice litter of puppies. The danger of inbreeding is the possibility of doubling up on faults, hereditary or otherwise, in two dogs that are very closely related unless the back breeding of the dogs involved is known.

The choice of a sire for your first litter is quite often the nearest who is suitable, because Griffon stud dogs are not easy to find. I was very lucky when I

31

started breeding Griffons because Mrs Deborah Gaines and Miss Tessa Gaines were then living in Essex. They were both very helpful and their advice and encouragement were invaluable to me.

The pregnancy

It is not easy to diagnose pregnancy in a Griffon. It can be done professionally if you ask your vet to examine your Griffon: some vets can confirm a pregnancy three weeks after mating. Nowadays, many use a scanner for pregnancy testing. If you prefer to wait and see, about four weeks after a successful mating the female should begin to fill out in the lower rib area. This will be noticeable when she is lying relaxed on her back. The vulva may not have returned to its normal size and her teats may still look enlarged from the season. When you are convinced that all is well and your Griffon must be in whelp, her food should be increased gradually and given at more frequent intervals, as a female heavily in whelp should not be presented with one enormous meal a day. Attention should also be paid to whether she is receiving enough vitamins and calcium. Towards the end of the pregnancy a bitch may prefer to eat just meat, without the addition of biscuit, meal or powdered additives. During pregnancy a bitch can be exercised normally until she becomes heavy at which time it is also advisable to see that she does not get jostled by other dogs or attempts to jump on and off chairs, particularly the latter which is liable to jar her body.

By the eighth week the whelping box should be ready and your vet telephoned to warn him or her of your impending litter. The hair around the bitch's teats should be trimmed off so that, when the puppies are born, they can find the teats easily.

It will be noticed that, although rough Griffons do not moult, their coats do become loose after a season which makes it a good time to strip the female if she has not been mated. However, if the female has been mated it is better left, so as not to disturb her while she is carrying puppies. About a fortnight before the expected arrival of puppies, the hair on the expectant mother's tummy area should be carefully trimmed off, cutting around the teat area with the greatest care.

Whelping boxes

On the grounds of hygiene and economy, I prefer to use a solid cardboard box for a bitch to whelp in, and a fresh, slightly larger box once the family has arrived.

The first box needs to be small enough for the bitch to get a purchase on the sides, which helps her when she strains and seems also to comfort her. Then, when she

'Come on, kids – dinner time!'

Starbeck String of Pears with her five puppies.

has been neatly tidied up and is complete with her family, a box lined with a Vetbed (a fleecy, super-absorbent lining), large enough for the bitch to stretch out comfortably but not so large that her babies can stray too far from her and get cold, is ideal. Cardboard boxes can be replaced as they become soiled and the puppies grow larger. In summer, if the weather is too warm for Vetbed, a thin piece of foam-backed carpeting, which can be bought as an oddment from a carpet shop, is useful.

Some breeders organise their whelping preparations in their bedrooms so that they do not have to sit up at night and the bitch is kept very quiet in the days leading up to her whelping. Other breeders have dog rooms and use complete whelping boxes and runs, which can be obtained at shows and elsewhere. I have the mixed blessing of a very large kitchen where the dogs sleep, so I prefer to have a small portion partitioned off by a wire pen with a curtain draped around for when the time comes for the bitch to live in the pen with her puppies. This gives her some privacy but keeps everything as normal as possible. I give her a large cardboard box, cut down to a comfortable height and lined with newspapers and a blanket, that can be quickly removed once whelping commences and until then used as her personal sleeping quarters.

The whelping

Most bitches go off their food just before whelping, but this is not always reliable. To be really technical, a bitch's normal temperature is 38.5°C (101.4°F); when it drops to about 37.2°C (99°F), whelping is imminent. Some bitches scratch around their bedding a few days before the onset of labour but when they really start whelping they become noticeably uneasy and may shiver or be sick.

As soon as regular contractions start the time should be checked because, provided all is well, the first puppy should be born within two hours. If the bitch is distressed and not getting on with the procedure, the vet should be telephoned at once for advice. There are many reasons why a bitch may need professional help: a dead puppy, a puppy presenting wrongly or an over-sized puppy, not to mention uterine inertia, meaning that the bitch cannot produce her puppies without help. I would suggest that any novice breeder should have a knowledge-able person with them or within easy call, because the first litter, or for that matter any whelping, can be nerve-racking.

A smooth bitch, newly-whelped.

Some bitches manage quite well unaided, but Griffons are short-nosed, so sometimes need a little assistance. If a bitch cannot bite quickly enough through the membrane in which the puppy arrives the result can be a dead or choking puppy. It is essential that the breeder can take care of any situation that might arise.

I always help a bitch who is whelping as a matter of habit, taking each puppy as it arrives, checking its mouth for mucus and giving its back a good rub to dry it and to make sure it is breathing well. Then I tie the umbilical cord in two places with a double thickness of cotton and cut between the two. Before tying I press any blood in the cord back towards the body of the puppy. Today, the advice from some quarters is to do absolutely nothing about tying the cord, so I would recommend asking your vet for advice on the subject.

Some breeders let their bitches follow the age-old custom of eating the after-births. My own vet is opposed to this practice, so I do not allow it. While the bitch is whelping I put the puppies into another box with a warm hot water bottle to keep them warm, and I give the puppies back to the dam when she wants them between births.

Cleft palates

I check that the puppies do not have cleft palates before giving them to the bitch to suckle. I have never found a puppy with an abnormal palate, but there is always a possibility of malformation, so checking is necessary.

Cleft palates are a very controversial subject. Many experts think that they are caused through a lack of essential vitamins in early pregnancy, namely A and D. As previously mentioned, novice dog breeders will find it advisable to make sure that their females are having an adequate amount of vitamins in their diet to ensure healthy puppies, which will hopefully also help to combat the incidence of cleft palates.

There are other opinions concerning the cause of abnormal palates. Geneticists say it is an inherited factor, and there are claims that the fault is to be found in certain lines which, if doubled up, cause the problem. Whatever the cause, I was interested to hear of a bitch who, having produced a litter of puppies all with cleft palates, was subsequently mated to the same dog and produced a litter of normal, healthy puppies. One cannot know what might happen in another generation if it is an inherited factor. A doctor at the University of California suggested, following experiments with rats, that cleft palates were caused by an acute deficiency of folic acid at a critical period of pregnancy. There could be many and diverse reasons for any given abnormality, none of which depends on a single issue.

Resuscitation

During whelping, a puppy that is difficult to get going or is breathing badly can often be revived by putting it into warm water up to its neck for a short while and then drying on a warm towel. Unlike some wild or domestic animals, which must feed first for survival, the prime requisite of a new-born puppy is warmth. A puppy

A rough bitch with her litter, 12 hours after birth.

that appears white and flaccid cannot be revived, but one which is blue and flaccid can sometimes be revived successfully by the method described. Any abnormal puppies should be put to sleep painlessly as soon after birth as possible.

Delayed whelping

For a novice breeder, a veterinary check is advisable during the first 24 hours after whelping, in case there is another puppy tucked away in the uterus which, even if born several hours later, will be all right. If there is a dead puppy inside the bitch, without proper attention she will become ill and die. Also a placenta could be left behind, necessitating an injection of pituitrin to evacuate it from the bitch, followed by some sort of antibiotic.

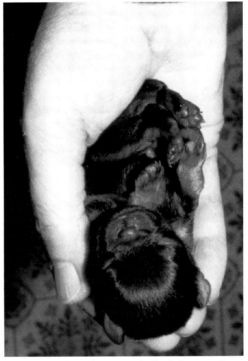

A very small newborn pup. Sadly, fading puppies sometimes have to be put to sleep.

An example of a bitch whelping normally, but overdue, is as follows:

07.40 pm: Commencement of whelping.

09.40 pm: First puppy arrived, weighing 140g (5^1/$_2$oz).

10.20 pm: Second puppy arrived, weighing 140g; the puppy was born rear end first and was in a very messy condition.

01.30 am: Third puppy arrived, messy and very weak, no time spared for weighing. The puppy had warm water treatment.

02.20 am: Puppy improved.

02.45 am: Puppy started to feed.

03.00 am: Fourth puppy, weighing 113g (4oz). Again born rear end first, filthy and with a mouthful of mucus to clear.

04.30 am: Fifth puppy arrived, weighing 127g (4^1/$_2$oz), no problem.

04.50 am: Everyone happy, but I have lost an afterbirth. This was soon retrieved.

05.00 am: Whelping over and I can relax with a cup of coffee!

Comment on the above whelping: The puppies were very dirty because the placentas were beginning to break up because of the lateness of delivery, but a

Caesarean operation was avoided by a few hours. All the puppies survived. The bitch continued in good health and was back in the show ring four months later, winning a Reserve Challenge Certificate.

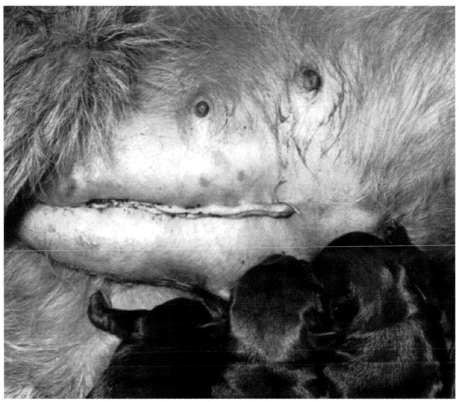

Puppies feeding happily although the dam has had a Caesarean operation.

Caesarean

There are several reasons why a bitch might need a Caesarean operation. When it is recommended, take your bitch to the surgery without any hesitation, together with a lined cardboard box or basket, and wait until you are allowed to see her again. Take also an extra cardboard box with a blanket and filled hot water bottle in readiness for the puppies. When you are a more experienced breeder and not inclined to panic, you may be offered the opportunity of helping with the new puppies, which can give you a small share of the satisfaction vets must have after a successful operation. Do not be disappointed if you are not allowed to help, since it is not accepted veterinary practice.

On arriving home with a bitch and puppies, tidy the bitch up as well as you can around her nether end with some cotton wool and settle her down with her puppies in some fresh bedding. Throughout the post-operative period it is wise to keep the bitch with you. Never leave her alone while she is still under the influence of the anaesthetic. If you cannot watch her all the time, ask someone to sit in for you until she is completely awake and has accepted her puppies.

Aftercare

'Zara' (Cleevecloud Czarina) and pups.

When the whelping is completed, I put the bitch and puppies onto a Vetbed where, after a drink of milk and some raw mince if she wants it, she can curl up with her family undisturbed. A few hours later, with the puppies safely penned away from the other dogs, I carry the bitch into the garden to allow her to relieve herself. This process has to be followed for a few days, because a bitch will seldom willingly leave her puppies even for a short period. Naturally, while she is away from them no other dog must be allowed anywhere near the babies.

During the first few days after the bitch has returned to her own nursing area, I feed her on plenty of raw butcher's mince and milk. If the bitch seems a little short of milk for her puppies, I give her some Welpi or Lactol (commercial brands of milk food preparation for bitches and puppies with all the essential ingredients for their welfare), gradually returning to a plentiful diet including milk and eggs. If the bitch is to be confined in a pen, there should be an area where she can lie down out of the reach of the puppies when she wants to rest.

The very minimum of time between litters should be a year, to allow the female to regain her strength and shape so that, when mated again, she can produce healthy puppies. The exceptions to this rule are if the litter is very small or if a longer rest or no further breeding is planned after the second litter. Many exhibitors only mate a bitch when they want a new exhibit to show.

Eclampsia

Eclampsia (more commonly known as milk fever) must be watched for in all nursing bitches because it can very quickly prove fatal. If at any time during the first three or four weeks after whelping, a bitch seems distressed, breathes rapidly, is constantly sick, trembles a lot or perhaps starts to stagger as she walks, contact your vet immediately. No time must be lost if a bitch is to be saved with an injection of calcium. It should be noted that eclampsia can also occur a few days before a bitch actually whelps.

Betty, a seven-week-old puppy.

Hand-rearing puppies

Should the breeder have the great misfortune to lose a bitch for any reason it is possible to raise the whelps on a milk replacement food. Raising puppies by hand is a matter of complete dedication to them until they are well on their way and beginning to eat at four weeks old.

From birth until about three weeks, puppies are unable to cope with their own bodily functions and have to be helped, a damp tissue taking the place of the dam licking her puppy. This means that the puppies have to be kept within constant ear shot so that they can be attended to when they squeak for help. Newborn puppies have to be kept very warm to prevent hypothermia and fed every two hours, day and night, for 10 to 14 days, depending on their weight gain and development. When I had an orphan litter to raise I kept the puppies on a blanket in a cardboard box warmed with bottles of not-too-hot water. As they grew I enlarged the area so that they could crawl on and off the well-covered hot water bottle whenever they wished to do so. I bottle-fed the babies with Welpi, mixing fresh at every feed and making sure that the hole for the puppies to suck through was neither too large nor too small.

After two weeks, feeding times for orphan puppies can be extended to every three hours during the day and four at night, again depending on their development. By the time the puppies are four weeks old they should be fed every four hours and sleep six to eight hours at night. Thereafter they should be raised as a normal litter.

It is a good idea for any breeder to obtain a bottle and teats suitable for small breed dogs, because any puppies that are a little weak on the dam can improve tremendously with a few days supplementary feeding.

One of the orphans I had to raise (eventually a happy matron) would occasionally, whilst sleeping, suck part of her blanket and make 'puddings', as a puppy will when nursing from its dam, from the rest of the blanket. It is extraordinary to watch and rather sad to realise just how much a puppy must miss a normal upbringing for it to have so much effect on the adult dog.

Docking

The question of tail docking is a controversial subject that has caused much discussion among breeders and owners in recent times. By far the majority of Griffon breeders are in favour of docking, and the novice breeder should consider the following points:

- Most potential owners will expect to purchase a Griffon with the traditional docked tail.
- A dog with an undocked tail may have no success in the show ring. (According to the Breed Standard, the tail is *customarily docked*.)
- Docking is a simple operation far less likely to cause problems than the removal of the dew claws, which is essential for the dog's comfort and future well-being.

Provided it is done correctly, docking does not impede a puppy's appetite for any longer than it takes for the operation to be completed.

The law now states that docking has to be carried out by a vet, whereas previously many breeders docked their own puppies. Unfortunately, many vets are now opposed to docking. However, many breeders, like me, are members of The Council of Docked Breeds (see **Useful Addresses**), an organisation set up to help breeders and vets who are prepared to dock. Along with other advice, this organisation provides members with a list of vets who approve of docking and are willing to

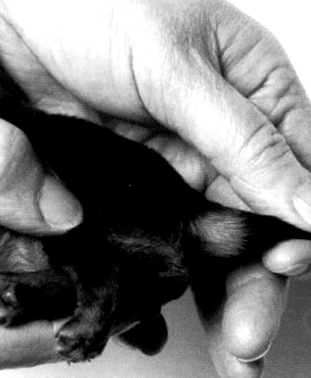

The light marking indicates where the vet should dock.

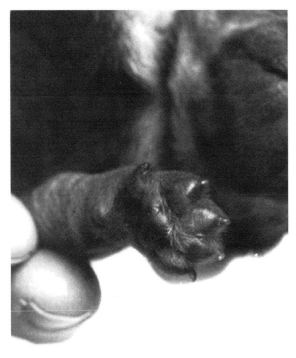

Dew claws need to be removed.

help you carry on in the tradition of your breed.

In case the vet is not very familiar with the breed, it is a good idea to show him or her exactly where to dock. When you turn the puppy over, you will see that the tail is a very dark colour, turning to a definite brown as it nears the body. If the tail is docked just before the brown colour begins, it should be the ideal length for a red Griffon. This marking also applies to Yorkshire Terriers, which is interesting in that it perhaps confirms their relationship in early Griffon breeding. In black-and-tan puppies the marking is usually where the red colour begins and the black ends.

The dew claws of the puppies need to be removed and, although it is probably more difficult than docking, breeders are allowed to carry out this operation them-selves. However, if the vet is coming to dock your puppies' tails, it is probably a good idea to ask for the dew claws to be removed at the same time.

Raising puppies

During the first few days of life puppies do not require much attention, apart from checking that the bedding is clean and the puppies warm enough. If any of the puppies are weak they may need to be placed onto the teats by hand. Particular attention should be paid to a very weak puppy, or it might die from dehydration. As previously mentioned, weak puppies can benefit from a few days of supple-mentary feeding.

At 10 to 14 days puppies open their eyes and at three to four weeks they begin to look for solid food, sometimes attempting to feed with their dam. At that time, I offer the puppies raw minced beef softened by a little hot water and cooled to a suitable temperature, or a mixture of Welpi milk and Farleys Rusks. Usually the meat is more acceptable because puppies are already consuming quantities of milk. During the introductory period puppies eat very little; they mainly lick it off each other's faces and their dam obligingly finishes the food and cleans the puppies. Next comes the messy stage when puppies require four meals a day and fall into

A three-week-old litter.

their food accidentally, play in it and generally cause havoc every time you feed them. However, as the puppies progress they despatch their food almost before you can turn around.

The early general care of Griffon puppies is also very important. Puppy housing should be sufficient for them to be able to move about but not so large that they can stray from the dam and get cold. As the puppies grow older and wish to relieve themselves without the aid of the dam, an exit from the box should be made for the puppies to go in and out to a very small run during the day. The area of the pen in which the puppies are allowed can be increased as they grow and the pen, whatever size, can be left open as soon as the puppies are strong enough to find their own way back into their sleeping quarters.

Puppies' nails need cutting at between two and three weeks old and again between four and five weeks old. At the latter age I also trim with scissors around the shape of the puppies' feet and trim off the hair under the pads, which helps puppies get well up on their pasterns when they start to move about.

In rough Griffons the hair from the eyes to the stop, which is just above the nose, needs to be kept short so that it does not impede the dog's eyesight. It is

Puppies soon become lively and full of mischief.

known as the fan because it is cut to that shape away from each eye. The hair around the tail end of the puppy needs constant checking; it becomes dirty, sometimes even blocking the anus. It is surprising how quickly this can happen, so it is wise to keep the hair trimmed well away from the anus.

When they are five to six weeks old I give the puppies a worming dose of Antepar or a similar preparation, which I obtain from my vet. The dosage is three to four drops to a puppy, given in a salt spoon. They usually like the taste and helpfully lick it off the spoon. I repeat the dose 10 days later. It is possible to worm puppies earlier if it seems necessary but only under veterinary supervision. The standard dosage for Antepar is 1ml per 2.3kg (5lb) body weight.

Recovery of the dam

Meanwhile the dam should be encouraged to spend more time away from her family until she returns only when she wants to suckle or play with her puppies. By eight weeks she should be sleeping away from her puppies and her milk should be drying up if not completely dry. Bitches vary in their lactation period; some lose interest in their puppies around six weeks after their birth, while others cheerfully suckle them when, if anything, it is only a teaspoonful of milk they have to offer!

After weaning the bitch should be in as good condition as before she was mated, except for the need for her mammary glands to flatten up into her body. By four months after the birth of a litter, the dam should be back in top show form.

A family group of red rough Griffons.

The Show Puppy

Jemerald Jasper, aged 10 months, with his dam, Jemerald Coral Delight, aged 3 years.

The average size of a Griffon litter is three to four puppies. A breeder may be unfortunate enough to have only one puppy from a brood bitch or find (as I did several years ago to my amazement) a bitch whelping nine puppies. To select one puppy, or possibly two, to keep and prepare for show is not as easy as the novice breeder might think. Puppies can change immensely as they develop and it is a fortunate breeder who possesses what is known as an eye for a puppy, which means they can visualise fairly accurately the changes that may occur during the first 12 months. The bewildered novice may sometimes wonder why on earth a particular puppy was initially selected.

Affixes

First of all, perhaps it is worth saying something about registering your puppies and the choice of an affix.

An affix is used to differentiate your kennel from any other by using it in front of the name of every puppy you register with The Kennel Club. According to the 1982 regulations, application to register your own affix has to be made to The Kennel Club on a form giving a selection of three possible affixes in order of preference. This selection must not include the names of places or prominent people, nor must it resemble an affix already registered. The chosen name is published in *The Kennel Gazette* for possible objection before The Kennel Club ratifies its choice. The cost of an affix can be paid either annually or for life.

In most cases, if you buy a dog, you can apply on a Kennel Club form to use your affix as a suffix on the end of the dog's original name.

It is a responsibility of Griffon breeders to register all their puppies: this used to help to keep up the allocation of Challenge Certificates (CCs) in the Griffon rings. Although it is no longer a criterion, it does

The finished product:
CC record holder Ch Dorelove Jimmy Mac (57 CCs).

provide a true record of Griffon breeding. No dog can be shown unless it is registered with The Kennel Club – a further reason for breeders to register their stock.

Coat and colour

The most popular coat and colour to breed has always been the red rough. Now the red smooths have caught up in the popularity stakes and, remarkably, classes have been seen recently where smooths have been predominant in numbers and successes.

Apart from a few specialist breeders who breed only red smooths, the majority breed a mixture of rough- and smooth-coated puppies in each litter. This is because of the dominance of colour in the red smooths. A red rough dog or bitch can vary in colour from wheaten to mahogany; the red smooth is usually a more stable colour of deep red and is used periodically to breed to its opposite sex in red rough to improve the colour of the progeny. Strangely enough, mating a red rough dog to a red rough bitch can produce all rough-coated puppies, a proportion of each coat, or even all smooth-coated. A smooth-coated dog mated to a smooth-coated bitch normally produces all smooth-coated puppies.

In the rest of Europe the two types of coat are not allowed to be bred together and are known and exhibited as separate breeds: Griffon Bruxellois and Petit Brabançon (see Chapter Two). However, this method of segregating coats does not find favour in Britain, Australia, New Zealand or the USA. Whether in Britain it will ever do so, as in the numerically large breed of Chihuahuas, is a matter for the distant future and depends upon stability of good colour in the red roughs.

The Breed Standard

Before making any serious decision about which puppy (or puppies) to run on with a view to showing, the exhibitor should refresh his or her memory by re-reading The Kennel Club Breed Standard. This is reproduced at Appendix A for easy reference, and you should consider whether there is a puppy in the litter being raised that comes near to the perfection described.

Ten-month-old Jemerald Jasper learning to 'show'.

Temperament

As soon the puppies are old enough to come out of their enclosure for a short while, I set aside a period of time every day when I sit on the floor with them. I then allow them to run around me and over me as they please while I observe their behaviour. It is necessary to watch how each puppy reacts to you and to strangers visiting your home. An extrovert puppy will greet everyone with enthusiasm. The playful six- or seven-week-old puppy who rushes around in ever-decreasing circles, puffing and panting with its own self-importance, is a puppy to keep an eye on for its future potential. So too is the puppy who has enough confidence in itself to feed with its tail straight up. This same puppy may later assert its right to an entire feeding bowl, making it necessary to have a separate dish for each puppy by the time they are about 10 weeks old. The quiet, friendly puppy, while ideal as a companion and pet, is not likely to excel itself in the hurly-burly of the show ring, particularly in indoor showing which requires tremendous confidence on the part of the puppy if it is to be successful.

Conformation and movement

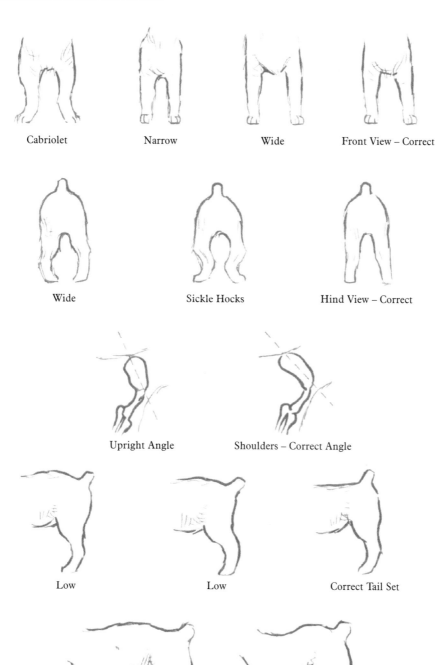

Cabriolet   Narrow   Wide   Front View – Correct

Wide   Sickle Hocks   Hind View – Correct

Upright Angle   Shoulders – Correct Angle

Low   Low   Correct Tail Set

Roach back   Dips to Shoulder

After temperament I take a much closer look at conformation (the physique of a puppy) and movement. These two attributes go hand in hand and culminate in soundness. If a puppy is built well it should move well, because it will have the correct set of shoulder, the balance of body and strong hindquarters to make it do so, unless for some reason there is a lack of co-ordination in the puppy.

Type

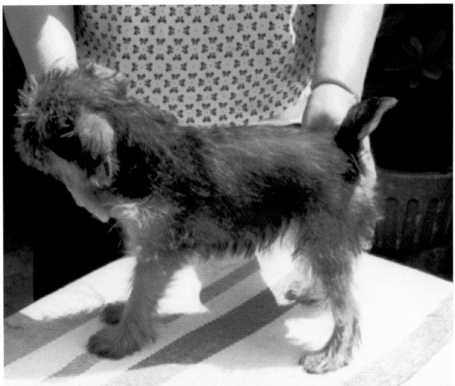

The body should be level along the back, with a well-rounded rib cage.

Type must have careful consideration: it incorporates all the above features. Every breed has its own characteristic temperament, without which you lose type. However, in my opinion, all the attributes one looks for go together. Nobody wants to show or breed from a dog, no matter how good, if it is not sound in every respect, so all its features must be given careful consideration. A puppy should have a good broad head, the nose set well back and the chin up, to give the quizzically alert expression. The eyes should be large and dark and there should be plenty of space between the small neatly-set ears, so that the puppy's forehead does not look narrow. The body should be short with sloping shoulders, and level along the back with a well-rounded rib cage. A medium length of neck is desirable (not the length of neck required of a terrier) and a high set tail and strong legs. The whole impression should be that of a smart cobby dog whose body measurements appear the same from point of shoulder to croup (point of tail) as from point of shoulder to the ground. Personally, I do not think it detracts from the female if she is fractionally longer in the back than the male. The average exhibitor likes to be able to breed from the stock they show and it does make breeding more viable if the female is suitably built to be able to carry puppies successfully.

From puppy to dog

It is easy enough to analyse all the points one would like to see incorporated in the puppy hopefully bound for the show ring, but not so easy to breed that puppy. You may well find that if you have a good point in one puppy, a different good point in another puppy and so on you would have the perfect puppy. Take comfort: we all look for perfection over the years of trying to improve on the breeding. Novice breeders may be confused by the head requirements of their Griffon puppies. It is nice to have a good short nose placement, but not at the expense of turn up. Griffons are not a 'head breed'; what goes on behind the head is every bit as important, the head is just part of the general attributes of a dog. In the past, the Continentals described the Griffon Bruxellois as having a *tête de singe*, head of a monkey. That effect can still be given with a slightly lower nose placement, provided that, most important of all, there is the lay back and turn up of the lower jaw that is an essential part of Griffon type. It takes around two years before the head of Griffon is fully developed, giving plenty of time between puppyhood and the adult dog for an overall improvement to have been made.

The movement of puppies can be very erratic. When a puppy is moving steadily it should turn a leg neither in nor out as it comes from you or goes towards you: in other words, movement should be straight and even in appearance. If you experience difficulty in assessing movement, it is a great help to ask somebody to lead your puppy in a circle and up and down while you watch how the puppy moves. A further good exercise for the novice breeder/exhibitor is to spare the time to watch other people's dogs in the show ring.

There can be quite a variation of size among Griffon puppies: some are

A five-month-old black puppy.

larger and longer in the leg while others are much smaller and more cobby. In the show ring there can be problems for either type. The larger puppy, because of its immaturity, may look a little long and run up in body and therefore may not do very well or be worth showing at all until 10 to 12 months old. On the other hand, the small cobby puppy who appears very mature could be ready for the show ring at six months old. The position of the two puppies can be reversed the following season. The immature puppy, like the ugly duckling turning into a swan, can blossom into an elegant dog, perhaps a little larger than the absolute ideal but still square as the standard demands. Conversely, the ultra cobby little puppy who may have done very well in junior classes can go over the top and become too heavy in the shoulder or show other failings when mature. However, there are many small youngsters who go on winning well and become champions at an early age and there are also many gangly youngsters who are put up in the show ring because judges recognise their potential.

To sum up: study of puppy behaviour can only be a generalisation, as there is always the exception. A shy puppy may turn out to be a super puppy when it reaches the show ring, while the bold puppy of which you are justly proud may collapse in a crumpled heap, making you wish the ground would open up to swallow you and your embarrassment.

Training for show

To be a credit to you the puppy finally selected to show must be properly trained before its début. A puppy should be accustomed very early on to wearing a collar and lead; some puppies take great exception to the indignity of their freedom

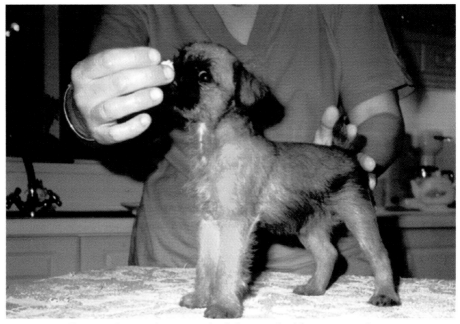

Show puppies must become used to being examined from a very early age.

Dozmare Dulcima, owned by Miss M Downie.

being curtailed by a lead, but they soon learn to accept the situation as one of the many quirks peculiar to humans which they must obey – a somewhat stubborn little puppy can turn into a self-assured champion.

With the encouragement of titbits, the puppy soon learns the art of standing still, upright and confident on the table for a prospective judge to examine it. Some puppies need steadying more than others on a table. Some will show freely, while others need the confidence of the owner's hand close to them. Training periods should be of short duration so that the puppy remains happy and willing to cooperate.

The puppy also has to learn to sit quietly in a show travelling box. A box put on the floor for the puppy to play at going in and out is the easiest way to accomplish this. Eventually the puppy will be quite happy shut in the box for short periods. This training avoids any traumas if you leave the puppy for a short time when you are travelling to a show and also helps to get the puppy into the habit of being left in a bench cage. Years ago there was a tendency among some exhibitors to keep their dogs at home in very confined quarters. This is detrimental to a puppy and ought not to be considered by the novice breeder.

Two or three months after it has been inoculated some exhibitors take a potential show puppy to a local ringcraft class to acclimatise it to mixing with other dogs and then, when it is between six and eight months old, to a small local dog show. Other exhibitors prefer to rely on their own home training of puppies, who make their first public appearance at a championship show.

A word of warning to all novice exhibitors at shows: the exhibitor must be constantly aware of their exhibit's safety, never allowing it too near another dog and always watchful that a large dog does not approach his or her little dog too closely for any reason, friendly or otherwise!

Preparing the coat

A puppy's coat will need tidying up a good six weeks before it is launched on its show career. I usually do this when the puppy I intend to show is four to four-and-a-half months old because, if I think a puppy is suitable to show early, I take it with an adult dog for company at six months old.

To prepare the coat, I place the puppy on the dog table and, after making a fuss of the puppy, I remove any hair that is sticking out from the body and legs. The hair which needs removing is often lighter in colour, remnants of puppy undercoat. The hair of the fan around the eyes should be checked to make sure it is short and neat. The hair from above the eyes to the front of the ears and sometimes from the back of the nose needs a careful strip to thin out any light hairs. Be careful not to get too carried away with the enthusiasm of stripping if you are showing the puppy fairly soon after it is eligible to enter the show ring.

At the show

If I may take a light-hearted view of the manner in which people show their dogs, you will notice that some exhibitors are compulsive coat groomers; the judge barely has the chance to look at the dog before the exhibitor is at it again, brushing away as though life were dependent upon it. Other exhibitors give the impression of being quite surprised to find a dog on the other end of the lead. Worse still are those who ignore the fact altogether and walk around the ring completely oblivious of their exhibit. You will also find cheery people who seem to think the show ring is the best place to chat with friends, those who bemuse their dogs with too much attention and, lastly, exhibitors who glower at the hapless judge, daring him or her not to place their exhibits!

In effect the rapport between exhibit and exhibitor can be a source of pleasure for the participants and the onlookers at the ringside. If the exhibitor inspires confidence and encouragement, the dog will walk out well and show itself to advantage. It is permissible to pick up your dog while you are waiting for it to be examined individually and walked out. However, it is well to be sure that your dog is standing correctly before the judge turns from the judging table to walk down the line of exhibits and make his or her final assessment.

Griffons are required to stand naturally with their tails at least half way up. There is a school of thought that says 90° is correct for the tail carriage, while others prefer the tail carriage showing straight up. The guiding requirement is that the exhibit must look happy. It is not correct to get down to a Griffon to make him stand well. This is known as stacking in the breeds where it is the accepted procedure, but with Griffons the naturally happy stance is required for perfection of type.

Junior Warrant

A very promising youngster of show standard can hopefully be shown through to a Junior Warrant from The Kennel Club. These are far from easy to obtain but well worthwhile. It means winning 26 points in basic breed classes between the ages of 12 and 18 months. The points are awarded as follows:

- A first at a Championship Show where there are CCs for the breed: 3
- A first at a Championship Show where there are no CCs for the breed: 1
- A first at an Open Show: 1

When the required 26 points have been obtained, the applicant has to write to The Kennel Club for a Junior Warrant Application Form or collect a form from a Kennel Club stand at a Championship Show.

Ch Dozmare Sprite in victory pose.

Showing

Mrs P Cuming judging Griffons at the Southern Counties Show, 1983. Photo: Hartley

To the uninitiated, showing opens up a whole new world that they may never have known existed, and it can be an immensely interesting hobby.

Types of show

Griffons being walked around the ring at a show in Sweden.

Shows are held all over Great Britain. At the lower end of the scale are Exemption Shows, sometimes held in conjunction with a local fête or flower show; at the exalted end are the Championship Shows, of which Crufts is the one most people will have heard, because it is advertised nationally and featured on television.

All shows come under the auspices of The Kennel Club and their rules are law to all exhibitors. No dog is allowed to be shown unless it is registered with The Kennel Club. The only exceptions are Exemption Shows, where unregistered pet dogs may be shown by special permission of The Kennel Club. In the pedigree classes of an Exemption Show a dog may not be exhibited if it has won a Challenge Certificate (CC).

At Exemption Shows there are a few mixed classes for pedigree dogs and the rest are fun classes, such as The Dog with the Longest Tail or The Dog Most Like Its Owner. All you have to do is take your dog along and enter it in the appropriate pedigree class. In the ring you are given a numbered card to pin on yourself and, with the other owners and dogs, you walk around in a circle for the judge to watch. The dogs are lined up and examined individually, and then walked up and down for the judge to assess their movement. It is all very light-hearted and a good way for both owner and dog to learn about showing.

A little further up the scale are the Limited and Sanction Shows, for which you have to enter from a schedule a short time before the show. The classes have various restrictions, such as entrance limited to members of the society running the show, and a grading restriction according to what the exhibit has previously won. Again, at these shows dogs that have won CCs are not allowed to compete.

Next are the Open Shows. As the name implies, these are open to any exhibit shown in its appropriate class. Each class has some sort of handicap, varying from age to number of awards won. Open Shows always used to be benched, which means that when you send in your entry you also have the cost of a bench (if it is a big dog) or a cage (if it is a small dog) to pay for; this makes for comfort for the exhibits and the public can view them. Alternatively, the benching cost would be included in the entry fee. Today this is not always done because of high costs and difficulty in obtaining benches. Some organisers of Open Shows are allowed by The Kennel Club to run their shows without benching.

Ch Fennymore Spankin' Good Time. Photo: John Hartley

Championship Shows are held over two to four days, catering for several thousand dogs, and an exhibitor can compete for the coveted CCs (Dog and Bitch) in their own breed to progress towards making up a champion. An exhibitor competes in a class or classes suitable to the exhibit being shown. If an exhibit wins a class, the dog then competes with all the other first prize winners for the CC and Reserve CC. The second prize winner of the Open Class is sometimes called in to compete for the Reserve CC. The winner of the CC competes with its opposite sex for Best of Breed (BOB), who then has the honour of representing its breed in the Group Judging. The Group Winners subsequently compete against each other for Best in Show (BIS) on the final day of that particular show.

The various Groups are as follows: Hound, Gundog, Working, Toy, Terrier, Utility. The Griffon Bruxellois is a Toy Dog, and is therefore shown in the Toy Group.

At Championship Shows there are CCs and Reserve CCs to be competed for. To become a champion a dog has to win three CCs under three different judges. A Reserve CC does not help towards making up a dog unless for some reason the CC winning dog is later disqualified. Once an exhibitor has received the honour of CC under one judge it is not considered etiquette ever to show the same dog under that judge except at a Club Show or Crufts.

Shows are advertised in *Dog World* and *Our Dogs*, where addresses of Show Secretaries can be found and schedules applied for. Championship Show entries close about six weeks or so before the event, so exhibitors have to plan what shows they want to enter well in advance. The new exhibitor will see from the schedule that there are some eight to twelve classes for Griffon Bruxellois. The cost of the first entry for any one exhibit is currently £14–£17 and subsequent entries in the region of £2 (1997 prices).

The entry forms for Championship Shows may look a little difficult to understand, but they are quite straightforward to fill in. It is a good idea to double check that you have entered your dogs in the correct classes before sealing and posting your entry, remembering that a puppy may not be shown until it is six months old. A week before the show, exhibitors receive admittance cards with bench or cage numbers printed on and a pass to let them out of the show ground at the end of the day.

From April to the end of September, the Championship Shows are held out of doors, many on permanent sites, such as the Scottish Kennel Club Show held at the Royal Highland Showground, the Midland Counties Championship Show held at the County Showground Stafford, the Welsh Kennel Club held at the Royal Welsh Showground, and Richmond held on Ascot Race Course. At all the Championship Shows there are wet weather arrangements, so judging continues either in the showground buildings or under canvas if it rains.

Preparing for the show

To prepare for a dog show, the exhibit's coat should be tidied up, its nails cut or filed and it might need a bath. The decision to bath depends on the state of the coat. If it is long and what is termed *on the blow* (meaning it will soon need stripping) it is wiser not to bath the dog, because it may look as though it lacks outline.

Show equipment

Griffons are penned in wire cages for which the exhibitor will need a blanket for the puppy or dog to lie on, plus a curtain which is hung on three sides of the pen to keep the draught out and act as a backcloth to the exhibit.

The exhibitor will also need to take to the show a water bowl; the parrot type plastic beakers that fit on to the door of the cage are very useful and can easily be bought from a show stall. Brushes, comb, a towel and a feeding dish will also be needed if you are travelling far. I usually take my own bottle of water and some people take milk. Speaking from experience, ladies may require a few extra personal

Ch Ardtighe Nerine of Kettleden. Photo: Thomas Fall

things with them in their show bag, such as a change of shoes and extra sweater in case the weather is unkind. Similarly, should there be a chance of the show day turning very warm, a change of lighter clothes. This may all seem an unnecessary nuisance, but these extras are indispensable if you are 200 miles from home and wet, cold or, on those rare occasions, even hot!

Travelling to the show

Dogs stretching their legs on arrival at a show in Sweden.

The majority of show exhibitors drive vast distances to venues. Some exhibitors share travelling expenses with friends and their dogs, while others may take caravans and stay on the showground the entire length of the show, usually exhibiting dogs on more than one day. For non-drivers, or those who prefer not to drive long distances, there are the dog coaches. Luxury coaches run in some areas and their organisers' addresses can be found in Championship Show schedules, or you can enquire at your local dog club or ringcraft class.

Personally, I was quite appalled by the thought of travelling with a lot of noisy dogs. However, although the journey may take longer, it is a very relaxed way to travel. The dogs seem to enjoy their day out and barely a sound is heard from them, except perhaps a snore! For the newcomer to showing it is an excellent way to become acquainted with fellow exhibitors.

Depending on where the show is held, departure can be in the very early hours of the morning. This makes a travelling rug on a coach an absolute necessity, because it can be very cold even in summer at that hour of the day, particularly if you are travelling to the North. On arrival at the showground, it is advisable to take your dog for a walk in the area allocated for exercise before benching your exhibit.

Judging

Judging starts between 9.00 am and 10.00 am and continues through the day, culminating in the Group Judging around 4.00 pm. Exhibitors are allowed to leave the show when judging has been completed, usually about 3.00 pm.

To the large kennels, showing is part of their business. It is all done very professionally by people who show many dogs, all beautifully presented. For the small breeder/exhibitor or the amateur 'one dog' owner, showing is great fun and should not be taken too seriously. There is a tremendous sense of achievement if you win a prize card but, if you do not, there is always another day, another show. It is a good thing to remember that most exhibitors go home without any awards. There are some exhibitors who are never very successful but go on from show to show, enjoying the companionship of their dogs and friends alike.

Judges vary considerably in their opinions and have various preferences in areas such as type and size. If they all agreed with each other, the show scene would be boring. It is the enthusiasm and bonhomie of most dog folk that make dog showing a popular sport.

A new exhibitor arriving at a ring where Griffons are to be judged will find fellow exhibitors settling themselves down at the ringside to watch the classes, many of them with their dogs beside them in show boxes or on their laps awaiting their particular class. When a class is called, the exhibitors take their dogs into the ring and are given an exhibit number card by the ring steward who checks that everybody is present. The only exception is if the ring numbers are left on the cages for the exhibitors to take to the ring, where again the numbers are checked by the ring stewards against the list of exhibits they have for that class.

The judge may take a general view of the class or look at each individual dog before asking for the dogs to be walked round in a circle. Then the dogs are lined up again and the judge examines each one on the table before asking the competitor to walk his or her dog in a triangle across the ring for the judge to assess the way the dog moves. The exhibitor may also be asked to move the exhibit straight up and down before returning to the other exhibitors. It is quite in order for the exhibitor to pick up his or her dog while other dogs are being looked at and play with the dog to keep its attention. Having made the individual assessments, the judge will return to the line-up to make the final selection. All dogs should be standing freely and alert. The judge may make an exhibitor walk out again, or make noises to attract your exhibit, which is done particularly by 'all rounder' judges and not always appreciated by Griffons. It can even lose you a place in the line-up if your dog ignores the judge.

It is as well for a novice exhibitor to make sure he or she is not over-shadowed by another exhibitor. An exhibitor should not hesitate to ask for a little more space if they feel their dog may be put off by the closeness of another dog. Some dogs show better if you have a titbit in readiness to offer while others show better without being distracted by food.

The novice judge

Judging is an honour and a privilege; an honour to be asked by a show executive and a privilege to be in a position to examine fellow exhibitors' dogs at close quarters.

A judge has to remember as he or she surveys a line of dogs that all the exhibitors have paid high entry fees and may have travelled a long distance to obtain his or her opinion of their exhibit. Therefore every dog, no matter how poor-looking, is worthy of as much care, attention and assessment by the judge as the most outstanding exhibit. It is also worth remembering that the people who sit at the ringside, many of them dog breeders of long standing, will know most of the dogs and be well aware of their good points and possible failings: these people will in their turn assess the capabilities of the judge.

In recent years there has been a marked change in the length of time it takes for an exhibitor to graduate from showing to judging a breed of dog. Since the shortened space of time, some exhibitors are eager to spread their wings and adjudicate. Others may still like to mull over a few thoughts before they take to the centre of the ring.

The Griffon Bruxellois can be a little uncooperative when asked to stand on a table in a show ring. Some have a marvellous penchant for looking awkward, backing off, or sinking in the middle of the back. Nevertheless, Griffons need to be handled gently and sympathetically. Puppies especially may be very sensitive, and could be ruined by a heavy-handed judge. The judge should not try out any possible veterinary expertise. An over-zealous examination, particularly of the back and hindquarters, could inflict damage on a small dog.

After careful and judicious handling, a judge can confirm his or her assessment by paying the very greatest attention to how the exhibit moves around the ring. A free-moving dog, showing balance and co-ordination, should confirm its construction beyond all doubt.

Some experienced judges are inclined to place young exhibits on their future potential. However, strictly speaking, the judge is there to place the dogs in order of merit on that particular day. To avoid possible pitfalls, the novice judge should adhere conscientiously to what is required and carefully study the Breed Standard of the Griffon Bruxellois or any other Toy Breed that he or she has the honour of appraising.

It should be unnecessary to say that a novice judge should not be at all swayed by who is on the other end of a lead when judging the exhibits. Do not assume that dogs shown by a well-known exhibitor must always be outstanding. Such selection can reveal the judge's own inadequacy. Mistakes can be made; even well-known breed judges will admit to an occasional error of judgement. But as long as the novice judge gives a totally unbiased opinion, he or she will obtain the approval of experienced members of the breed and a good entry at subsequent judging appointments.

To summarise judging, a famous 'all-rounder' judge once said: *Most people when judging make the mistake of concentrating on the bad points instead of looking for the greatest number of good points.*

Aspiring Championship Show judges have to keep all their judging books and marked-up catalogues in all the breeds they judge at Open and lower grade shows to fill in The Kennel Club Application Form and pass as a Championship Show judge.

Crufts

The show season culminates in mid-March at Crufts, held at The National Exhibition Centre, Birmingham. To be eligible to enter in the Breed Classes, your exhibit must have won certain prizes during the current year at a Championship Show in either Minor Puppy, Puppy, Junior, Post Graduate, Limit or Open Class. A dog that is already a Show Champion is not required to have won further prizes in a current year and neither is an exhibit listed in *The Kennel Club Stud Book*.

Ch Dozmare Distinctive at Crufts, 1996. Photo: Freeman

Some exhibitors are a little blasé about exhibiting at Crufts and quite unimpressed by the aura of the show: however, I think there is a certain magic about Crufts. From the time I wait, sometimes with the wind and swirling snow blowing into my face, for the coach to appear over the hill until I return late in the evening, win or lose, I know it will be an exciting day to remember. The bustle when the exhibitors pour out of the coach – showboxes, show bags, big dogs, little dogs and one or two children – all making their way to the security check before entering the vast halls, strangely quiet in the early morning. Then when you have settled your dogs, you greet other arrivals and perhaps have some breakfast. Almost imperceptibly the halls become a hive of activity as more and more exhibitors arrive. Then judging commences. Visitors fill the National Exhibition Centre and English becomes only one of the many languages you will hear during the course of the day. The stalls with their vast array of goods

My first Griffon with a nine-pup litter. Although she was no oil painting, one of her grandsons became a champion.

make it an Aladdin's cave where you can buy anything from a valuable work of art to a range of kennels.

After the show you meet up with your fellow travellers once more and then search for your coach amid a great gathering of coaches from all over Britain. At last, thankfully, you are bundled in and on the way home, watching the lights of Birmingham recede into the night as you ride off into the countryside.

Past quotes from well-known exhibitors:

Griffons make all the rules. Long may they continue to do so.

Mr Stanley Dangerfield

Start with a good foundation – behind many successful kennels is a large bitch.

Mrs Olive Lewis

The Griffons well earn the sobriquet of The Connoisseurs Breed.

Miss Marjorie Cousins

Life is but a hollow sham, in which a Griffon plays no part.

Mrs Handley Spicer

We do not all get the CCs we deserve, but let us deserve the love the Griffon gives us.

Mrs Gwen Davitt

To travel hopefully and smile.

Miss Ann Tyler

Oh where oh where has the terrier-type temperament gone?

Mr Keith Langston

Take the roughs with the smooths.

Mrs Rathbone

There is as much bad in the best of us, so much good in the worst of us, that there's no reason why any of us should speak ill of the rest of us.

Quoted by Mrs Eileen Street

To labour with zest and to give of your best,
For the sweetness of joy of the giving.
To help folks along with a hand and a song,
Why! There is the real sunshine of living!

Miss Ursula Gregory

Jemerald Jasper with owner/breeder Jenny Kearney at Crufts 1996. By kind permission of *PetDogs*.

Griffon Colours

Ch Bowerhinton Pennistar of Tunlake. Photo: Thomas Fall

If a study of present-day red Griffon pedigrees were made it would not be too difficult to find the name of a black Griffon introduced somewhere along the latter end of the pedigree. It has also been found, as a result of some old pedigrees coming to light, that some of the supposedly black introductions were black-and-tan. Presumably the mixing of colour was done to improve the colour of the red roughs. Today breeders are either totally opposed to the mixing of colours or in favour of the occasional mating between dogs of different colour.

In breeding black-and-tan Griffons, red or black Griffons have been introduced now and again because the nucleus of black-and-tan breeding bitches is so small. It is considered that red with black-and-tan gives a better coloured progeny for future mating. The cross with black can cause a poor-coloured tan marking. But whatever the pros and cons of colour breeding, it is not recommended to the novice Griffon breeder, although the more experienced may regard colour breeding as an added challenge in their breeding programme.

The red Griffon

The Cleevecloud clan. Photo: Susan Hamlett

The red rough Griffon is the most popular colour and coat among show people and pet owners. Red Griffons are by far the most numerous in the breed.

Some exhibitors prefer the rough-coated dog because it is possibly the more glamorous, and skilled trimming for presentation can cover the odd inadequacy. The pet owner usually finds the beard very appealing and delightfully different. Nevertheless, the red smooth has an ever-increasing following, both as a pet and for show. Mrs Barbara Murray (Operastar) holds the record for making up smooth champions. True, nothing can be disguised on the smooth exhibit but, despite that disadvantage, smooths compete well against their rough-coated counterparts. Mrs Dovey Kirk, who died in 1992, was another devotee of the red smooth. Her Speedwell Griffons were very successful in the show ring but, strangely enough, it was her red rough, Speedwell Prosper, who proved to be one of the most success-ful by siring nine champions.

Colour is always a vexed question in the rough-coated dog. It varies from a sandy colour through to the designated clear red and on to brown and brindle. I did once hear of a puppy being registered as blonde!

It has become fashionable for some people to say that dogs in the ring today are not as good as they were 20 or more years ago. It might be true in a few cases but, across the board, there are some lovely dogs both in the show ring and in pet homes. Naturally, there is always room for further improvement, which is what breeding is about in all the colours.

Ch Hunters Melody of Gregtoi. Photo: Thomas Fall

During the mid-1980s and early 1990s there were two outstanding dogs in the show ring, both of whom broke the record formerly held by Ch Hunters Melody of Gregtoi. Mrs Ann Fenn's impressive dog Ch Starbeck Crystal Rainbow (see page 124) has been a great modern promoter of the Griffon Bruxellois at Championship Shows. Over the years he won eleven Toy Groups, six Reserve Toy Groups and three Best in Shows (BISs) at all breed Championship Shows, plus one Reserve BIS at an all breed Championship Show. He also won a United Kingdom Top Toy Competition and was a Pedigree Pet Food Champion Stakes finalist, as well as winning other awards in the course of his career. Ch Starbeck Crystal Rainbow died aged almost 12 in 1996.

Mr Neil Swan and his wife Gwen hold the Dorelove affix. They too have produced an outstanding dog in Ch Dorelove Jimmy Mac (see front cover). He was

Starbeck Corsair. Photo: Hans Bleeker

Leading Griffon from 1987 to 1993 and holds the British record with 57 CCs. He was Reserve BIS at Windsor Championship Show in 1992, BIS at the UK Toy Dog Show in 1993 and a Group Finalist at Crufts in 1992 and 1993. Among his other awards were six Toy Groups at general Championship Shows and numerous BISs at breed Championship Shows, plus other leading general awards.

Other exhibitors and affixes include Mrs Pat Crick and her Shenden Griffons, successful in Britain and overseas. Pat's current champion is Ch Shenden Viking. She also breeds and successfully exhibits Sealyhams, as does Mrs Phoebe Cuming with her Polrose Sealyhams and Griffons.

Miss Mary Downie has the well-known Dozmare affix and bred the 1996 Best of Breed (BOB) winner at Crufts, Ch Dozmare Distinctive (see page 61), owned by Mr Graham Lee.

Miss Morwenna Marshall holds the Menwinnion affix, and formerly held the Mountwhistle affix with her mother. Mrs Elizabeth Lunn has the Bobenut affix, Mrs Susan Hamlett the Cleevecloud and Mrs and Mrs Norman have the Keidrey affix. Mr and Mrs Burke have the Markath. Mr Peter Hawkins, who has the Petrahawk affix, imported some stock from Sweden to add to his kennel a few years ago, and Mr Howard Ogden (Beauview Griffons) imported from Australia.

Over the border in Scotland are Mr and Mrs Connor's Inchlee kennel and Mrs Margaret Reid's Kettleden Griffons. A newer breeder exhibitor is Mr James Finlay

Ch Operastar Mignon and Ch Operastar Fledermaus. Photo: Thomas Fall

Three Shenden reds on a bench. Photo: David Paton

with his GilderOak Griffons. Across the sea in Northern Ireland Mrs Joan Saunders, who I believe is now semi-retired, has the Ardighe affix and Mr Ivan Thompson has the Lareve affix.

Back in England, Mr and Mrs Groves have the Maricoat affix, Mrs Margery Day the Polcot and Mr Ron Henny the Wilicot affix. Mrs Posnett has the Dreda affix, Mrs Bentley the Sirosador (formerly Doredona) and Mr Bill Bradbury, a long-time exhibitor, now breeds Griffons with the Bilchry affix.

Mr Stephen Bardwell has the Stewell affix and is also well known in other breeds, including Yorkshire Terriers, Norwich Terriers and Airedales.

Mr David Guy has added Griffons to his kennel with the Donzeata affix. Mrs Mandy Suggitt has the Aptrick affix, Mrs Burt the Sijasa and Mr and Mrs Lee the Supadon affix. Mrs Littmoden and her daughter Mrs Wendy Spencer share the Wendlett affix and Mrs Bull has the Carlton affix.

The most successful kennel not specialising in one colour is that of Mrs Mary Ann Mercer who, with her husband Peter, came into Griffons from American Cocker Spaniels with the Fennymore affix. In a comparatively short time Mary

Ch Marquant Miss Scarlet. Photo: Carol Ann Johnson

Ann built up a very successful breeding programme, making up several champions, including Ch Fennymore Code Name Gertie (Leading Bitch), and becoming the Leading Kennel in 1990, 1991 and 1992. After a few years without exhibiting, Mrs Mercer returned to the show ring in 1995.

Meanwhile, Mrs Alison Price and her Marquant Griffons have become very successful in the last few years, making up champions and becoming Leading Kennel in 1994. Alison's top exhibit is Ch Marquant Miss Scarlet, who has 27 CCs to her credit – a terrific record for a female Griffon.

Ch Fennymore Code Name Gertie.

These and many more, too numerous to mention by name but to whom I must apologise for leaving them out, are the breeders of the red Griffon Bruxellois.

The black Griffon
by **Maureen Higgins (Jaydean)**

Ever since Griffons were first imported into England there has been a small section of devotees who have striven to keep the blacks within the breed. To these past breeders must go our thanks and gratitude for, without their dedication, this colour would not be in the strong position it holds today and, in my view, the breed would be the poorer. A good black Griffon in full bloom is a beautiful sight. It has not

Jaydean First Love at five months. Photo: J Phoenix

71

Ch Bowerhinton Black Baron, the first smooth black champion. Photo: Thomas Fall

always been an easy task to keep this colour going without inbreeding, especially in the early days, as at times numbers have been so few. Reds have been, and still are, carefully used in breeding programmes. Today I would say that blacks are in a stronger position than at any time in the history of the breed, now that we have different lines and families on which to base our future litters.

The first black champion, a dog, Ch Nofa Gollywog, was born in May 1916. For those interested, he was from Line AT, Family 19. He was bred by Miss Cookended and owned by Mrs Alder. Nofa sired three black champions out of Joyette of Sunningdale, one being Ch Othello of Causeway, born November 1925. There was a lapse of seven years before the breed had another black champion. This was again a dog, Ch Gerrards Chough, born in 1932 and sired by Corbeau. The Gerrards are still in evidence today, as Miss Thomas took over the affix from her mother, but in later years it has become a red kennel. The breed had to wait 34 years before the first black bitch gained her title; she was Ch Skibbereen Amoret, born in 1950, and soon followed by Ch Toymore Lady Jet, a bitch born in the same year. Later I will list all the champions in order of gaining their title, as space does not permit a more detailed account.

All the above-mentioned were rough. In Norma Wiley's *Book of Champions* a red rough dog imported from Belgium, Ch Bruno, has the earliest authentic date of birth: 28 February 1895. So, from that date, it took breeders 61 years to produce the first black smooth champion: Ch Bowerhinton Black Baron, by Toymore Black Magic, born in 1952, and gaining his title in 1956. He was bred by Mrs M Fearfield and Mrs J Squires and owned by the Hon Mrs Stillwell. The only other smooth to achieve the distinction to date is Ch Gay Cavalier of Kirkmarland, born in 1964. Both these dogs are the same line (AT) as Ch Nofa Golliwog, but from different families.

At first blacks and black-and-tans were not allowed to compete with reds. Because of this a separate club was formed to promote an interest in these colours. In the Christmas edition of *The Illustrated Kennel News* dated 12 December 1913, Mrs Handley Spicer (later to become Lady Handley Spicer), writing about the black says: *I believe a Club to forward its interest is in the course of formation.* Later, *The Illustrated Kennel News* of 2 January 1914 says, *We hear that the proposed Club for black Griffons has been successfully carried through, it will be known as The Griffon Belge Club.*

The officials of this Club, who were also committee members of the Griffon Bruxellois Club, were: Secretary – Mrs Charters; President – Mr T Whaley; and Treasurer – Mr Shambrook Saunders. At that time they had 30 members. The Griffon Belge Club was mentioned in the 1914, 1915 and 1916 Stud Books but not the 1917, so it seems that when all colours and coats were allowed to compete together this club was disbanded. Happily the interest remained strong enough to ensure that, since the first black champion, some lovely specimens have always existed. At times these have been rarities, only one or two appearing in a whole entry. Today the position is different and more and more often we can see a class consisting of only blacks or where they outnumber reds. At a recent club show 21 blacks were entered, which I think must be an all-time record. Now they are becoming more uniform in size, shape and quality. I would also venture to say that, generally speaking, black coats are better in texture and colour than the reds, but still we get judges who will penalise a less-than-perfect black coat while overlooking a soft, light red or a red carrying lots of black. Some judges cannot or will not see a black – definitely a case of colour prejudice – and I believe this is not peculiar to Griffons but also happens in other breeds.

Cynjon Cover Girl.

Cynjon My Lucky Star at 10 months. Photo: Carol Ann Johnson

Here are some recent affixes of kennels that have either started in blacks or added them to their kennel: Ailsa, Aptrick, Bajalon, Bolmacs, Chosendale, Cleeveview, Cynjon, Dajela, Forshaw, Jaydean, Krandon, Lareve, Manmist, Stopford and Wendlitt. There are others who have just bred or acquired their first blacks who will, hopefully, fall in love with this colour and continue.

As a tribute I will mention the Manmists and their breeder Mr Ernie Hall. Ernie's untimely death came just as his years of devotion to his favourite colour were beginning to bear fruit. He made up his first champion, a bitch, Ch Pottle Black Petal, in 1983. She was sired by Manmist Leprechaun, a black smooth who, in my opinion, should have been used much more than he was. From Petal, Ernie bred the black rough Manmist Marcus, who won two CCs and sired two English champions, Cynthia Howard's Ch Cynjon Glamour Girl and my own Ch Jaydean Cole Porter. In Sweden, Marcus' son is Swe Ch Cynjon Don Juan and his grand-daughter Swe Ch Jaydean Night and Day. She is out of Manmist Mandragora (see page 76). Such a pity Ernie didn't see all this; he would have been so proud.

Here is a complete list of Black Champions in order of gaining their title, followed by year of birth:

Dogs

Ch Nofa Gollywog   1916

Ch Erebus	1925
Ch Othello of Causeway	1924
Ch Corbeau of Causeway	1925
Ch Gerrards Chough	1932
Ch Zadok of Fieldburcote	1947
Ch Bowerhinton Black Baron	1952
Ch Ruskinton Toby	1955
Ch Knight Errant of Gregtoi	1956*
Ch Black Boy of Beachart	1958
Ch Ruskinton Remy	1960
Ch Black Arrow of Gregtoi	1963
Ch Gay Cavalier of Kirkmarland	1964
Ch Skibbereen Black Magic	1972
Ch Krandon Jumbo Jet	1974
Ch Krandon Storm Warning at Blomacs	1977
Ch Jaydean Cole Porter	1985

Bitches

Ch Skibbereen Amoret	1950
Ch Toymore Lady Jet	1950
Ch Bramble of Edinample	1953
Ch Ruskinton Desiree	1957
Ch Bowerhinton Jenny Wren	1955
Ch Annabelle of Kirkmarland	1960
Ch Ettiene of Gregtoi	1960
Ch Skibbereen Lucetta	1963
Ch Glenalda Gigi	1963
Ch Concorde of Krandon	1972
Ch Pottle Black Petal	1978
Ch Cleeveview Calypso	1982
Ch Cynjon Glamour Girl	1986

* Gregtoi was the affix of the late Misses Gregory. It has now been protected by the Northern Griffon Club of which Ursula Gregory was Secretary for 35 years. Her sister Esther was Treasurer for almost as many years.

These figures are to the end of 1989. There have not been many black champions since then. Any there are will be listed with the others at Appendix C.

I cannot say that a good black coat should differ from a good red coat. Both should be harsh and wiry and both should have an undercoat, meaning that they should be stripped in exactly the same way, with finger and thumb. This is the ideal, but there are those in both colours who do not have an undercoat, and this is wrong. I have been lucky not to have one. I have bred one or two blacks who had

Three generations: Manmist Mandragora of Jaydean, Jaydean Hallmark of Aptrick
and Aptrick Silverload.

soft coats as puppies, but after two complete strips the coats have come through
harsh and never reverted to softness. In my opinion a soft black coat is much easier
to improve with quicker and longer lasting results than a soft red coat. Someone
once said to me, 'You can't see a black,' and this is never truer than when you are
stripping one. It is sometimes hard to differentiate between the top coat and the
undercoat, so occasionally your dogs end up with little bald, blue patches. Do not
worry: these cover in 10-14 days.

Another type of coat can be found occasionally in reds and blacks, and the
author tells me it is common in her black-and-tans. This is the flat tight coat that,
when stripped out, leaves a new, very short, hard coat. This is the exhibitor's
delight as the dog can usually go straight back into the ring without a break in his
show career.

One thing I do find different between colours: blacks grow more hair both
inside and outside the ear. This means that extra care must be taken to keep the
inside clear of hair to minimise the risk of ear infections.

There used to be two schools of thought in the preparation of this colour:
those who hand stripped and those who clippered. Those who clippered said that
this method gave a good texture and colour even for the show ring. To these I
would say that if a dog had a short show career it would probably work. However,
these days dogs can be in the ring for five to six years and I would think a coat
clippered for this length of time would deteriorate in texture and colour, as cutting
off the top of the coat and leaving in the dead roots would eventually turn a black
coat rust or grey and a red coat blond.

These are only my views on coats and intended for the novice; there are those
with much more experience than I. I will add that a good black coat should shine
from within and not from constant bathing.

I will end this section with a challenge, or perhaps a plea to all breeders of blacks: to produce the first black smooth bitch champion in the history of our breed in this country. This, along with the first black-and-tan smooth bitch, will complete the picture of our exceptional breed. But be they red, black, or black-and-tan, I hope that Griffons will grace this world for ever.

The black-and-tan Griffon

The rough with the smooth: Mahnyar Penny Black and Mahnyar Nightingale.

By their lack of numbers in the British show ring today, one would assume serious Griffon Bruxellois breeders disapprove or simply choose to ignore the black-and-tan colour. This is difficult to understand, as they are very outgoing dogs and most attractive, their ebony black coats and bright tan markings rendering them fascinating to breed – perhaps all the more so because the breeder has to wait for the depth of colour in the rough variety to materialise as the puppy matures.

It is true that black-and-tan Griffons are not easy to breed. There are very few lines, and breeders eventually have to mate back to red to avoid too much close breeding. If in the future more Griffon breeders choose to breed the colour the situation will

Ch Mahnyar Dragonfly. Photo: Christina Lees

not continue and we shall hopefully have lasting lines of black-and-tan Griffons for exhibition and as companions for people who admire the colour.

Black-and-tan Griffons have had a somewhat chequered history. They were originally exhibited in Any Other Colour (AOC) Griffon classes, which meant any colour but red. The colours included black, brindle, black-and-tan, blue and even grey, collectively known as the Griffon Belge. From reading very old critiques, one deduces that black-and-tan Griffons were sadly maligned. One particular judge who praised a black-and-tan exhibit qualified it with the words: 'Certainly not a Griffon Bruxellois!' Another judge who wrote about a black-and-tan exhibit said: 'What a pity it is not a red!' Small wonder a club was formed, although only of brief duration, to look after the interests of the AOC Griffons.

Despite such inauspicious beginnings, black-and-tan Griffons became popular and flourished quickly as the numbers of breeders grew before the First World War. Miss Bland bred up a line of black-and-tans from her successful kennel of Marland black Griffons. Lady Handley Spicer bred black-and-tans from her famous line of red Copthorne Griffons. Unfortunately both these lines faded and were apparently never bred together. Amongst other early breeders of black-and-tan Griffons were Miss A F Hall (Park Place), Miss A J Johnson (Sunnymead) and Mrs Cochrane (Witchampton).

Between the two World Wars, Mrs Cliff of the Irton affix was breeding black-and-tans, as were the Hon Mrs Ionides (Vulcan affix) and Mrs Mitchell (Lavenderway affix). Mrs Mitchell was the first breeder exhibitor to make up a black-and-tan champion, the rough-coated male Ch Simon of Lavenderway, in 1934. Present-day black-and-tans are descended from that champion and the Hon Mrs Ionides' Vulcan Menhisto. In 1938 the Griffon Bruxellois Club put on their first separate class for black-and-tan Griffons.

In the 1950s Mrs Eileen Street made up 12 champions, one of whom was the first rough black-and-tan female champion: Ch Skibbereen Vanta of Irton.

Miss Raphne Deck (Tunlake) who started to breed Griffons in 1947 has had a lasting effect on the breeding of black-and-tan Griffons. Many champions are descended from her line both here and in America. Miss Deck, along with Mr Desmond Gregory, was the most knowledgeable authority on the breeding and genetic peculiarities of the black-and-tan Griffon.

Mahnyar Bumblebee.

During the 1950s and 1960s several well-known Griffon breeders specialised or included black-and-tans in their breeding programmes: Mrs Winner (Wynworth), Miss Outram (Glyntirion), Mr and Mrs Davitt (Tumpfa), Mrs Bird (Incanton), Mrs D Harris (Stouravon), Mrs Farmer (Remraf), Mrs P Rathbone (Munjay), Mrs F Tuckwell (Dundry), Miss Cawley (Ringrose) and Mr D Gregory (Chosendale).

Mr Gregory came into Griffons from Fox Terriers in 1954 and he made up the second rough female black-and-tan champion, Ch Chosendale Pennicandy of Tunlake, bred by Miss Deck. Mr Gregory himself bred the first smooth black-and-tan male champion, Ch Chosendale Seamus, and he also bred and exhibited the rough black-and-tan male, Ch Chosendale Crispin.

Breeders who have fallen more recently for the black-

and-tan Griffon charm include Mrs Pat Wiggins (Andirion), Mr and Mrs J Wheeler (Sherway), Mr and Mrs Norman (Keidry) and myself.

Nevertheless, the British black-and-tan Griffon continues to be the Cinderella of the breed. It is possible that the difficulties of breeding the colour put would-be breeders off the project. The main problem is the lack of a good gene pool. This means it is not very long, once the breeder has been able to breed black-and-tans, before an outcross has to be considered to keep the line going.

Using a black-and-tan dog over a red female can, by British standards, produce some very heavily shaded colours. The alternative is using a black with a black-and-tan but this too can produce colours not acceptable in the breed. The progeny of a black-and-tan cross red mated back to another black-and-tan should produce a percentage of black-and-tans. In contrast, if you mate the progeny of a black-and-tan cross red back to a red Griffon you are likely to produce only badly marked reds, even if the red dog siring the litter has himself black-and-tan breeding in previous generations. However, mating in the same manner can produce a litter of clear reds. In the particular case to which I am referring there were five puppies. The only difference in the two matings was that the dam of the second litter was a black-and-tan smooth, whereas the dam in the former litter was a rough. The females were mated to different red dogs with black-and-tan behind them.

One red rough female from the smooth black-and-tan mating, in turn mated to a totally unrelated black-and-tan smooth dog, produced two red smooth puppies and one black-and-tan that died during birth. The same red rough female, in her second and last litter (by the same dog) produced two puppies, one red and one black-and-tan, after a Caesarean section.

When one does finally manage to mate black-and-tan to black-and-tan it is a delight to see a litter 100% black-and-tan. Black-and-tan mated together must always produce black-and-tans: a statement which has caused a little controversy in the past...

In Miss Marjorie Cousin's book *The Second Book of The Griffon Bruxellois* there is a pedigree of a litter of mixed, two chocolates, a blue and a red. The litter was purported to be from a mating of two black-and-tan Griffons.

Miss Raphne Deck wrote, and I quote from *The Griffon Bruxellois Bulletin* of Spring 1964: *I expect most members will now have Miss Cousin's great new book and if it were not so, I should not feel it so important to point out especially for those who wish to breed Black/Tans that the 'Pedigree of mixed colour breeding' is in error. The book was prepared for publication before we knew as much as we do now about Black/Tans, and I am sure that had Miss Cousins lived she would have queried the facts given her.*

Miss Cousins died in 1962 before the book was published in 1964. For there to be only one error in such a prodigious work on Griffon lines and families is in itself extraordinary. How sad that Miss Cousins did not live to see her book in print.

Miss Deck continues her very interesting article with the backing of a geneticist on colour breeding, and finishes with a very succinct remark to the effect that some people who do not know the true colouring of a black-and-tan can mistake a heavily-marked brindle for black-and-tan.

Once the breeder has been able to mate black-and-tan to black-and-tan he or she is still far from the ultimate success. When considering a puppy for showing, the *musts* of such points as conformation, type and movement all have to be considered before one actually gets to the colour of the puppy. Then can come the disappointments. The well-marked puppies are often not of show quality or either too big or too small. It takes time and perseverance to make the grade.

In the British Standard, while the red Griffon is required to be a clear red, the black-and-tan is immediately at a disadvantage because it is required to have rich tan markings. On the plus side, there is no actual directive on the deployment of the markings. In some Toy breeds the tan markings are very exacting. In one breed the exhibit must, amongst other things, have the thumb markings on the front legs. In another breed such a marking is a fault; the legs must be clear. The markings that I feel are absolutely necessary for show and breeding are the tan eyebrows, which add so much to the facial expression.

Breeders will find (although it is not easy) that they will acquire an excellent tan in their smooth Griffons long before they reach the same standard of excellence in the rough dog. I understand this problem is something to do with the genes generally in some long-coated black-and-tan breeds of dog. Conversely, the tan eyebrows are more difficult to obtain on the smooth.

A cluster of black-and-tans.

International News

(**PLEASE NOTE**: The following overseas articles represent the exclusive opinions and views of the respective writers.)

Australia and New Zealand
From notes by Mrs Mollie Grocott (Moerongi affix)

Griffons first went to Australia about 1909 but nothing much was heard of them until 1936 when at the Royal Melbourne Show the challenges were awarded by Mrs Dorothy Whitwell from England to Oliver of Marengo and Ch Gerrards Mayflower. After that, from the Griffon point of view, show entries decreased and did not resume in any number until after the Second World War when Mrs Madge Sheehan (Robinvale) was the first exhibitor to import and show her Griffons.

In New South Wales the first post-war imports appear to have been Chilkoh Toby of Campfield and Ch Rossington Fantome of Campfield. The latter was a daughter of the famous Ch Skibbereen Victor of Campfield. Mrs Sheehan won Best in Show (BIS) at Canberra in 1951 with Fantome, whom she apparently bought from Mrs Peggy Crawford, another early breeder who later turned to Pekes. In 1958 Mrs Sheehan won both the challenges at the Sydney Royal.

The next Griffon kennel in Victoria was Mrs Grover's Woodover. Mrs Grover was well known as the importer of Aust Ch Starbeck Copper Dance, a son of the record-holding Ch Hunters Melody of Gregtoi.

Mrs Joyce Pemberton (Vomak), who now lives in Brisbane, bred Griffons in Great Britain and has a record of more than 23 years of breeding and showing Griffons. Mrs Constable of South Australia is another of the earlier breeders: her affix is Colchester.

During the early 1960s Mr Thompson imported Gaystock Le Beau, but sadly did not allow anyone to use him. Around the same time, Dr Cunningham, a veterinary surgeon in Adelaide, imported about nine Griffons, amongst them Dubraw Drambuie, Griffjoy Gremlin, Nicki Noodles of Gregtoi and Harmony of Crossgate. Mrs Sheehan added to the imports with Bowerhinton Brandy Snap.

In Sydney interest seemed to have lapsed until Moerangi Meander, a New Zealand champion bred and owned by Mrs Grocott and a BIS at a Toy Show, went over on lease to Messrs Rigg and Gray. Meander was a grandson of Gaystock Le Beau from breeding effected before he left Great Britain. Meander won his Australian title, including Challenge Certificates (CCs), at the Royal. He returned to New Zealand and later went to Cape Town, where he quickly got his title and won well at a big show under Mr Owen Grindey. Since then the breed has slowly but steadily become more popular.

The first, and to Mrs Grocott's knowledge the only, Griffon Club in Australia is the Griffon Club of Victoria, established in 1975. The Patroness is Mrs Madge Sheehan and the first President was Mrs Scott. The club was started largely as a

Aust Ch Braganzar Noblesse. Photo: Michael M Trafford

result of the hard work and enthusiasm of Mrs Elsie Fulton (Melponty), who was its first Secretary. The first General Meeting was in 1975 and hardworking members were Mrs Beth Grover (Woodover), Mrs Thelma Roscow and Mrs Betty Merrick (Hagunn).

Aust Ch Braganzar Nestor.

In New Zealand the first Griffons were imported by Mrs Wilson and Mrs Brownson. La Parookh Butch in 1945 was the first, followed by Skibbereen Olivette, Skibbereen Teddison and Skibbereen Candytuft. These were followed by Joriemour Juliana, Ringrose Rinty and Gaystock Minette brought out by Mrs Wilson in the 1960s.

In 1967 I brought out from Gaystock Le Bruit Sec and La Vivacitée. Le Bruit Sec did not like showing but compensated by doing a tremendous amount for the breed in the stock he sired! 'Viva' did quite a lot of Group winning as well as having some lovely puppies. Since then I have brought out 12 others, amongst them the record-winning smooth in the United Kingdom, Ch Dozmare Sprite, bred by Miss Downie but campaigned all his show life by Mrs Wilde. At that time, he was the only smooth to have won a Group, which he did on two occasions. He did a great deal for the breed in New Zealand.

Another dog to make an impact was Starbeck Cristingle, bred by Mrs Fenn. He was the first Griffon in New Zealand to win BIS at the first Championship Show held in Melbourne by the Victoria Griffon Club. His children have also done their fair share of winning at shows.

A further dog who might be mentioned is NZ Ch Buka Tiger Moth of Moerangi, bred by the late Mrs Osbourne. 'Tigger' had won a Junior in Show at a

Toy Show and then lost an eye: however, despite this mishap, I made him up. He went on to spend some time in Melbourne with Mrs Merrick and won the award Leading Stud Dog at the Griffon Show. His daughter, NZ/Aust Ch Moerangi Gypsy Moth, has the record of being BIS three times at the Griffon Show.

Other notable winners are Mrs Canavan of Melbourne who won Best Toy at the Adelaide Royal under Mrs Pamela Cross-Stern and again under the same judge at our National Show, where Ch Moerangi Warlock, owned by Mrs Fowler, and a son of UK Ch Dozmare Sprite won Best Intermediate Toy and Reserve Toy. Another win at our National was in 1974 when Mrs Viner's Mauiti Humphrey, son of Gaystock Thistle of Mountwhistle, won Toy Puppy. The judge this time was Mr Carveth of Canberra. Ch Moerangi Marauder notched up a first for the breed by winning two Best Intermediates at all-breeds Challenge Certificate Shows.

Griffons have been brought over from Australia but I think a greater number have gone there from New Zealand to do well both in showing and breeding. Although I would like to see more Griffons in New Zealand, I would prefer them to remain more or less static in numbers than to be bred to such popularity as the Cavalier King Charles Spaniel, which sometimes, as the result of injudicious selection, retains only a vague resemblance to its breed.

All my Cavalier friends who have looked after or bought a Griffon are amazed at their intelligence and I have found that people become addicted to Griffons very easily. At various times I have had friends look after my dogs and the next thing is that they want one of their own!

The first bitch I had, bred by the late Mrs Wilson, was bought as a pet and was always at my side. Once when I was going away to stay she could not come with me because she was in season. Twice she climbed out of the kennel where I put her and sat by the car. Whilst I was away she was kept for the first week where she could not possibly get out. The following week she was moved in with a Cavalier from whose run she could have escaped if she had really tried. However, she made no attempt to do so until 10 days later and, when I came home, she was sitting at the gate waiting for me! Very sadly she was eventually run over and lies under a magnolia tree. The whole family was desolated. I wrote to Jane Wilson and told her of our tragedy and said I could not bear to have another. Within a week I had written again, asking when would she have some puppies as we could not bear to be without a Griffon.

'Busy', the one who was killed, had a mouth that kept her out of the show ring, but she worked well at Obedience

NZ/Sw Ch Moerangi Delusion.

NZ Ch Moerangi Copyright.

which was in its infancy here at that time. I could sit her outside a supermarket and she would stay like a lamb. However, I stopped doing this when I realised how very easy it would be for someone to snatch her up. Her successor 'Zeezee' gave everyone a shock when she won Best Toy and Best Puppy in Show at the same show, a feat which had never been attained by a Griffon.

The show season, as in Britain, runs through most of the year until a gap around Christmas, followed by another in June and July. The National Show is held in August. This is similar to Crufts and attracts an entry of some 3000 dogs.

During the early 1990s Griffons on this side of the world have gained in popularity and are at most shows. Caroline Gillies sent me out Moerangi Migrant who won well in groups and in show. Sadly he died this year from kidney failure. One of his daughters is now in the United States. Another import from the Marshalls of Mountwhistle was Mountwhistle Lucy Locket who came out in whelp to Ch Gaystock Tour de Force and produced a litter of seven. Her biggest winning son was Moerangi le Forte who had seven Juniors of Group and three BISs at Toy Shows. Sadly, he is also no longer with us. I have just landed Starbeck Crystal Spectre, a son of Starbeck Crystal Rainbow, who should be a great asset to the breed. The best thing for the breed is that Ch Moerangi Copyright won the first BIS at an all-breeds show by a home-bred Griffon. The Morrises and Whites in the South Island brought over nine pups from Mrs Merrick of Hagunn, Melbourne, and I am told that two of the dogs she brought from Great Britain are now in New

Zealand. The BOB at our National was a smooth bred by them from Aust Ch Marquant Mega Star. I believe the black rough is also here, Dajela Black Baron. My Moerangi Buccaneer was Reserve at the National.

Last year's National saw Moerangi Copyright win seventh out of 70 BIS winners at a special class and the year before Aust/NZ Ch Moerangi Smuggler was Reserve Toy under Mr Nigel Aubrey Jones. He has done very well for his co-owner Mrs Seymour, winning Best Pup at the Victorian Griffon Club Show, the following year not shown as I was judging, and the following year BIS at that show. He won CCs at all the Royals at which he was shown. Mrs Seymour is now campaigning a son of Starbeck Chevronaires who has had a BIS at an all-breeds show: Aust/NZ Ch Nouveau Graffiti, bred by Alastair McKinlay. He is out of Ch Moerangi Esprit, a daughter of Lucy Lockets. At this year's show BIS was Mrs June Owens Beagriff Minstrel, who had two Moerangi grandparents. Best Bitch and Reserve in show here was Denis Montford's import Aust Ch Gaystock la Marraine. Denis also imported Ch Gaystock la Femme Fameuse and has some interesting pups already.

It is interesting that Mr Howard Ogden, who judged the Griffon Show Victoria 1990, should choose to take back to Great Britain a bitch by Ch Moerangi Smuggler from a bitch by Aust Ch Moerangi Copper Twist out of Braganzar Naidah, who goes back to Moerangi Gerda and NZ Ch Gaystock le Brut Sec. Thank you, Howard, for endorsing my British imports. Denis bred her grand-mother, so the imports from Great Britain have gone full circle. It is interesting to note that the Griffons with which Jill Seymouir has been most successful all go back to stock brought in by Denis Montford from Gaystock, except Aust Ch Starbeck Copper Dancer. I could not get to the show that Howard Ogden judged as my son was flying a vintage airplane round New Zealand and I wanted to be in the country. Ian Pollock has had many group wins with Ch Moerangi Cardsharp, and a newcomer to the breed, Mrs Kim Butler, has just had a Junior of Group with Ch Moerangi Curlylocks, so she is hooked on the breed.

I am very proud that Copyright will hold the record of being the first Griffon bred and handled by the exhibitor to win a BIS at an all-breeds Championship Show. I think this has not been done in Australia yet, but with Denis Montford's imports it should not be far away.

Another area in which Griffons are making themselves felt is Agility. Janet Ritchie has won and been placed with Moerangi Harridan, a red smooth, who is a granddaughter of the famous Eng Ch Dozmare Sprite, whom I brought out in 1972 and who I think I am correct in saying is still the only smooth to have won a Toy Group in Great Britain.

We do not have a breed club here but usually have a Griffon Gathering at my home just before Christmas; last year we had 70 attend, and many of them smooths. They are gradually becoming entrenched here.

Sweden and Scandinavia
Mrs Gunn-Ell Sehlstedt (Walliant); updated 1996 by Christer Jernhake (Vendetta)

The first Griffons came to Sweden about 1910 and their blood-lines were mostly Belgian. In the beginning of the 1930s the breed became more popular and

Int/Swe/NZ Ch Moerangi Delusion.

English imports were shown and used at stud. During the 1950s and 1960s there was increasing interest in the breed and several English imports came over, amongst them Swe/Fin Ch Toymore Folly, the first black-and-tan to be seen in this country. Another famous dog was Int Ch Skibbereen Felix (by Ch Skibbereen Victor of Campfield) who unfortunately died young but did a lot of winning, including a Toy Group. Swe Ch Mousette of Campfield (a CC winner in England) was imported in whelp to Ch Skibbereen Brandan in 1949 and had a smooth son, Nordic Ch Competitor av Sano, who was the most famous smooth at that time. His name can still be found in many old Swedish pedigrees. Another dog who was used a lot at stud was the Belgian import, Swe/Dan Ch Jazz du Clos des Orchidées.

From 1961 several English imports came over to the Walliant kennels of Mrs Sehlstedt. Amongst them was Int Ch Belinda Molach who was a Group Winner and Griffon of the Year in 1967, and Eng/Int Ch Bowerhinton Billy Simon who was a Group Winner in England as well as Sweden and who sired many winners. Int Ch Dozmare Minimus and his smooth older sister, Int Ch Dozmare Marie Claire (by Dozmare Sprite), also had great influence at stud. Minimus left a litter behind in England and his son Buka Maurader (two CCs) also sired winners. Marie Claire was unbeaten in her sex in Scandinavia and was the dam of eight champions and two CC winners, a record still to be beaten for a Griffon bitch. Int Ch Skibbereen Strazda Hi'Style came over in 1976 and his beautiful top-line and tail-set can often be seen in his progeny. In 1980 Nordic Ch Crossgate Carfax was imported and became Griffon of the Year the same year. The same title was awarded to Swe/Norw Ch Polrose Prototype (by Eng/Am Ch Starbeck Chinrullah) in 1982 and he was also a Group Winner. The next year one of his Walliant sons won the title. Prototype's most famous progeny is Swe/Fin Ch Walliant's Ephraim who in 1984 became the first Swedish Griffon ever to go BIS at a Championship Show and he also won another Toy Group later that year. To date, 37 champions have been bred by Mrs Gunn-Ell Sehlstedt, who is the leading breeder in Sweden.

Another well-known breeder is Mrs Hedfors, whose affix is Backängen. Her foundation bitches carried the old Swedish blood-lines and she has used Enavant and Barratelle dogs to them and bred several outstanding Champions. Int Ch Otterbourne Otuto was imported by her in 1978 and has sired many winners. In 1981 she imported a female Griffon, Keidrey Eira, who became an international champion and won two Toy Groups during her career.

After Miss Forwood's death Eng/Swedish/Norw Ch Enavant Bastian was imported by Mrs Brunbäck in 1973. He won the Toy Group three times and was much admired over here. Int Ch Barratelle Golden Hoopoe also did a lot of winning a few years earlier, together with his kennel mate Int Ch Enavant Zeeta.

Black-and-tans are rare in Sweden, although there is now a growing interest in them. Blacks are not shown very often either but the imported dog Int Ch Jollicoates John O'Gaunt had a successful career and was Griffon of the Year in 1977. Most blacks in Sweden go back to Int Ch Black Dougal of Molach and Nordic Ch Kirkmarland Chief of Molach (both exported by the late Miss Stuart to the Walliant kennels) and their kennel mate, the smooth black bitch Swe Ch Shelvey Seashell.

In 1984 the red smooth Int Ch Starbeck Czigany was imported and became a

Swe/Norw Ch Cayata's Ikaros.

Five generations of bitches: (from right) Int Ch Belinda Molach, Int Ch Walliants Lucinda, Walliants Melinda, Int Ch Zamina and Lu-Lu-Belle.

milestone in the history of the breed. Though not excessively used at stud he is the leading stud dog of all time and is so far the sire of 25 Champions. His progeny excel in toplines, tail-sets and, like him, are beautifully balanced. Though Griffons are not often picked out in the Groups, several of his children have also succeeded in winning top awards there. One of his most famous sons is Int Ch Emhås Delphinium, considered by many authorities to be one of the best smooths in the world. Consequently he has attracted a lot of attention and was the Smooth of the Year in 1986, 1987 and 1988. Now his son, Swe/Norw Ch Yazoos Fredrik Åkare, is following in his footsteps and ruling the ring. He has recently won his first Toy Group at a Championship Show after having been picked out many times before and he was Smooth of the Year in 1989 and 1990. To date, 59 champions have been bred at the Walliant kennels, which is a record in Sweden.

Mrs Brunbäck owns a grandson of Ch Enavant Bastion, Int Ch Hostlers Halo-Bump (ex a daughter of Starbeck Chindit). He dominated the ring from 1985 onward. Halo-Bump is a top-class Griffon of outstanding type and quality. Two of his offspring have been imported into England by Mr and Mrs Hawkins and have done quite well at shows. A son of one of the Swedish-bred females was exported back to Sweden: Petrahawk Foxfire, who became a successful Swedish champion and is also the sire of champions. Swe/Norw Ch Cynjon Don Juan was imported in 1988 and is the sire of several champions.

Three roughs have dominated the scene so far in the 1990s. Griffon of the Year 1990 and 1991 was Swe Ch Notorious Muffin Man, bred and owned by Annika

Nyman. Muffin Man is by Ch Hostlers Heart-Breaker (full brother of Ch Hosters Halo-Bump, mentioned above) ex Starbeck Cornflower Belle (imported to Sweden in 1984 as the foundation bitch for the Notorious kennel). Muffin Man's full sister, Swe Ch Notorious Miss Muffet, is now with the Vendetta kennel.

Griffon of the Year in 1992, 1993, 1994 and 1995 (a breed record) was Swe Ch Moerangi Delusion, imported into Sweden by Siv and Christer Jernhake (Vendetta) from Mollie Grocott in New Zealand. He is out of two Moerangi dogs, but goes back to Starbeck and Gaystock dogs imported from England.

The third rough dog is Swe Ch Walliants Matador, bred by Gun-Ell Sehlstedt, owned and campaigned by Birgitta Olsson. He was Griffon of the Year in 1988 and has been shown ever since, usually finishing second or third behind the other two.

In smooths, Swe/Norw Ch Yazoos Fredrik Åkare (mentioned above) continued to dominate the scene in the early 1990s. However, he has now been retired, and his place has been taken by Ch Cayafa's Ikaros, bred by Birgitta Friman but owned and campaigned by Helena Rankleven (Rocanas). Ikaros is out of a daughter of Walliants Matador, Ch Walliants Natalina who, like her sister Ch Walliants Napolitana, is a very nice bitch. Napolitana has been Best Smooth at the club show a couple of times and both sisters have been Smooth of the Year.

Griffons from the Backängen kennel have continued to be quite successful in club shows in the 1990s, although they have not appeared so often on the top lists. The most notable of them have been Backängen's Nashville, Griffon of the Year in 1989, and two litter sisters, Backängen's Makösa Manic and Backängen's Marimba. A daughter of Marimba, Backängen's Piaf, has also been quite success-ful, finishing up as Best Rough in BIS-2 at the latest club show.

Swedish Griffons are considered to be of a very high quality, especially the roughs, and they are noted for their soundness. Swedish breeders have been very particular to breed from sound stock only. Almost all dogs have their patellas checked before being used at stud, so luxating patella is very seldom seen nowadays. Recently, a few breeders also started to X-ray the hips of their Griffons, but it is still too early to make any conclusions. There are Griffons in whom hip dysplasia is diagnosed, but they do not usually show any symptoms from it and live perfectly normal lives, so I do not think it is a big problem in the breed. In Sweden all Griffons are reg-istered with the Swedish Kennel Club and the registra-tions in 1983 were 99 roughs and 40 smooths.

All official dog shows in Sweden are organised by local

Swe Ch Ailsa Coruscate.

Swe Ch Vendettas Va E'Nu Detta.

kennel clubs belonging to the Swedish Kennel Club or by local clubs belonging to the Swedish Companion Dog Club to which the Toys also belong. The classification at these shows is always according to the Fédération Cynologique Internationale (FCI) system. This means that Bruxellois (red rough), Petit Brabançon (all smooths) and Belge (black or black-and-tan roughs) are judged separately. Nearly all judges are all-rounders or Group all-rounders. Only three judges who are or have been actively involved in the breed are authorised by the Swedish Kennel Club to judge Griffons: Brith Andersson, whose father Sven Olof Andersson bred Griffons under the affix Jockes; Siv Jernhake of Vendetta, authorised 1987; and Christer Jernhake, her husband, authorised 1996. A fourth person who could be said to have a special interest in Griffons is all-round judge Kenneth Edh, who owned a Griffon a few years back.

In view of the number of all-rounders involved in judging our breed I think the judges' conferences organised by the Swedish Companion Dog Club are very important to discuss the Breed Standard and the standing of the breed. Given the limited number of dogs shown at normal shows it frequently happens that dogs not really up to standard are awarded CCs and go on to become champions. It is said that it is up to the judge to withhold the CCs if the dogs are not of sufficient quality, but this does not always work with judges who perhaps only see the breed once or twice yearly when they are judging.

The breed club, the Swedish Griffon Association (SGS), organises a show of its own annually. This is an unofficial show, but it still attracts many more dogs than the official shows. The policy of the club when it comes to appointing judges has not been very consistent. Sometimes it has been seen as a training ground for potential judges of our breed, but sometimes well-qualified English judges or people involved in the breed in other countries have been invited. The latter approach is favoured by Christer Jernhake.

The Swedish Griffon Association (SGS) was founded in 1961 and therefore celebrated its 35th anniversary in 1996. In connection with this, work on a new Griffon book has been started, with the purpose of documenting what has happened in the breed since the previous Griffon Book was published in 1985. It is hoped that the book can be used to train new judges.

In Norway and Denmark Griffons are not seen very often. Danish breeders, and Finnish ones since 1988, are isolated from Sweden and Norway because of the quarantine laws against rabies but are allowed to show their dogs on the continent. The annual title of World Champion has been awarded to Danish dogs several times. Their blood-lines are based on Swedish and English dogs. Norwegian breeders have brought their dogs mostly from Sweden, though a few Gaystock Griffons have also been imported. The Swedish imported dog, Int Ch Amarillo (by Int Ch Starbeck Czigany), is the best-known, with a brilliant show career, even a BIS at a Championship show in the Netherlands. Probably he has achieved more titles than any other Griffon, as he so far can put 19 in front of his name: he is shown all over the continent.

Finland has become very strong in Griffons in recent years and is now quite up to the Swedish standard. With the importation of Mrs Parcerisa's Int Ch Gaystock l'Heros in 1978 Finnish Griffons really started to make their presence felt in Scandinavia. L'Heros has had the most wonderful career and is the highest winning Griffon ever in Scandinavia and has also turned out to be of great value at stud. Further back, dogs imported from the kennels of Lalarookh, Skibbereen, Buka and Starbeck are behind many Finnish dogs. Another well-known affix, in addition to the Huvikumpu one belonging to Mrs Parcerisa, is Cheerea belonging to Mr and Mrs Rönnholm who have bred reds, blacks and black-and-tans for many years with great success.

The future for the Griffon in Sweden is not easy to forecast. At the moment the interest in the breed seems to be on the decline numerically as some of the people who have been heavily involved for the past 20 to 30 years have either lost their interest altogether or cut down quite considerably, no doubt partly because of the docking ban introduced in 1989. In 1995 only 60 dogs were registered by the Swedish Kennel Club, and at general championship shows it is unusual to see more than a dozen dogs altogether.

With some perseverance in showing most Griffons can be made up, and the title of champion is by no means a guarantee for a really good specimen. Champions are not allowed to compete for CCs but have a class of their own, making it even easier to get the tickets. From 1990 there have been three sets of CCs: for red roughs, black and black-and-tan roughs, and smooths. In my opinion this will lower the quality even more, as competition in the Belge variety is poor and most judges far too generous in awarding CCs.

Because of the docking ban several Swedish breeders have given up breeding, and the loss of all their experience and knowledge in breeding Griffons true to type will, I am afraid, be disastrous for the breed. This makes it all the more important for those of us remaining to breed to the standard.

United States of America
Richard A Ball

Since 1899, when the first Brussels Griffon was entered in the American Kennel Club Stud Book, the Brussels Griffon has enjoyed a small but loyal following here.

In the early days of the breed in the United States most winning Griffons were imported from Belgium. Many of these foundation Griffons were imported by Mrs Olivia Cedar, who owned a pet shop in New York City and was also a well-known breeder and exhibitor. After the First World War, when the Brussels Griffon population was almost decimated in Belgium, the British flair for animal husbandry asserted itself in the breeding of Brussels Griffons. The vast majority of the winning Griffons in America today stem from British bloodlines. Breeders in the United States have done their share in producing top-flight specimens, especially where soundness and showmanship are concerned.

American breeders have realised that it takes more than just a pretty face to compete for high honours in the show-ring. Many American-bred Brussels Griffons move with such soundness and show with such sparkle that they are envied by many of the Terrier breeds.

By the end of the mid-1980s eight Brussels Griffons had achieved the coveted BIS award at all-breed shows in the United States, the first five American-bred and the last three imported from Great Britain:

* Ch Barmere's Mighty Mman, bred and owned by Miriam H Breed
* Ch Red Ovation of Wil-Daw-Cy, bred by Dawn Vick Hansen, owned by Jack Goring Jr and later by Mamie Gregory
* Ch Fuzzypeg Flim Flam, bred by Marie Yuhl, owned by Mamie Gregory
* Ch Wallin's Charlie Brown, bred by Ardis Wallin, owned by Sachiko Takada
* Ch Rosebud, the only member of the distaff side to reach this pinnacle, bred by Peggy D Hamilton, owned by Claire S Bradshaw
* Ch Gaystock du Tout Temps, bred by Deborah and Tessa Gaines, owned by LeRoy Love and Maxwell McQuillen and later by G & M Lewis
* Ch Gaystock Caster of Mountwhistle, bred by Nancy Marshall, owned by Mr and Mrs Lee Murray
* Ch Starbeck Chinrullah, bred by Ann Fenn, owned by Mrs A R Howard Jr

While American Griffon breeders and exhibitors maintain great respect for top quality British-bred Griffons, the words Imported from England are no longer the guarantee of success in the show rings of the United States that they once seemed to be. Today our American-bred Griffons compare favourably and can compete successfully with Griffons from any part of the world.

During the late 1980s a number of Griffons in the United States have become outstanding Toy Group and BIS winners. Leading the parade is Ch Starbeck Silken Starshine, top winning Toy dog in the country for 1988. His son, Ch Treyacres Zorro, is following in his sire's footsteps and is the top winning Griffon at this time. Several other Griffons are also winning in Groups and gaining BISs.

As a result of the ensuing publicity interest in the breed has soared. Many breeders have long waiting lists for show, breeding and pet stock at abnormally

Am Ch Cot'n'wd Cap'n Crunch. Photo: The Standard Image

inflated prices. New people are coming into the breed in unprecedented numbers, many with no previous experience in dogs. Some new breeders are doing irreparable harm to Griffons by arranging matings simply to produce puppies, with no thought as to the suitability of the pair involved. While our established breeders are producing many top-quality Griffons, these are being inundated in a sea of mediocre stock bred by inept novices and puppy farm type breeders.

Another stumbling block on the road to upgrading the breed is the fact that very few of the judges licensed to judge Griffons have more than a cursory knowledge of the breed. Evidence of this is the fact that one out of every five Griffons registered becomes a champion. There are not enough judges with the self-assurance to withhold ribbons from undeserving dogs. As a result, pet-quality Griffons become champions.

The two clubs catering for the breed, The National Brussels Griffon Club and The American Brussels Griffon Association, are doing everything possible to educate club members, so hopefully as time goes on the situation will improve.

One happy note is that the standard has been reformulated and, by a vote of the members of the parent club, the disqualification of the black smooth from being shown has been rescinded. This has been approved by the American Kennel Club. Such a change has been the goal of many of us over a long period of years.

1990s update by Priscilla Wells (Cot'n'Wd): Breeding and showing the Brussels Griffon in the United States presents the same challenges and rewards as it does the world over, simply by the uniqueness of our breed. The vast size of our country, along with our structured all-business attitudes, seem to have created a competition that stimulated growth in the need for presentation. Hence we are known for our talented professional handlers. However, for whatever reason, the owner/handler is on the rise, and very often seen in the Griffon ring, giving the professionals a run for their money.

When planning future shows, we collaborate with other breeders; our numbers are scattered so, if we do not do so, we will spend valued time, effort and entries just to find that we have the only Griffon entered. For this reason, we concentrate on those few Specialty gatherings, and try to make the most of them. Louisville, Kentucky in March is fast becoming the annual Olympics of dogdom in the United States, especially for Griffons, since it is our national Specialty. That weekend starts on a Friday, with numerous independent specialties and continues until Tuesday, with four independent all-breed shows. The grounds are spacious and very well organised, which makes for great atmosphere. The Spring 1996 Griffon Specialty boasted an entry of 120, and the event was judged by the noted Anne Rogers Clark.

The overall quality seems to be becoming better and, when the pedigrees of the winners are examined, usually will show the distinct influence of several past British imports through line breeding. I am thrilled to report a noticeable increase in showing Griffons with natural ears. (Since we are allowed to crop we have the best of both worlds, being permitted to do away with a problem if it presents itself.) The smooth also is making its way through the woodwork, although it remains a rarity here. I guess by their very nature they appeal to those weary groomers looking for an easy route!

As always in the United States the glory shines in the hands of some of our very talented handlers. And now, no less than ever, if you were to frequent any one of our many shows you might have the good fortune to see one of our wonderful little Griffons in 'full dress', strutting his or her stuff, and more than ever making it known to the world that they are, by rights, the Best In Show!

Belgium

Jan den Otter (v d Platte Belskes)

Belgium is the country of origin of the Griffon Bruxellois, but through the years England has put her stamp on the breed and quality. Without England there would not be a Griffon left in Belgium as all today's Griffon breeders in Belgium started with foreign lines. In these lines we find many dogs that go back to English stock from the 1960s. British breeders started to import Griffons from Belgium at the end of the 19th century and have established a strong type and improved the body of the Griffon.

In the early days there was a little rough-coated breed of dog in Europe from which several countries acquired their own local breeds. In Belgium the little working dog was bred with the ruby King Charles Spaniel and the black Pug, which was very popular at that time, giving it a short nose and also forming the red rough-coated Griffon Bruxellois, the red and black-and-tan Griffon Belge and the smooth-coated Petit Brabançon. In 1883 they started their Stud Book. The first registrated Griffon was Fox (LOSH 516).

When Hans Bleeker and I were planning the *Belgian Champion Book 1892-1994* we were allowed to copy all registered Griffons and their litters from the records at the Société

Belgian Ch Lotje. Photo: Hans Bleeker

Royale St Hubert (the Belgian kennel club). It's still possible to register a stray, whose offspring can be registered normally in the official Stud Book, the *Livre des Origines Saint Hubert* (LOSH), after three generations. In the early days they did not use an affix like most of us do now.

In 1888 Griffon and Skipperke enthusiasts joined together to form the Skipperkes Club et Club du Griffon Bruxellois. In 1892 the Griffon Bruxellois dog Marquis (LOSH:1933) (Fox ex Miss) became the first Belgian champion. In 1904 the Griffons had their own breed club and a year later organised the first international Championship Show for *Chiens de Dames, de Luxe et d'Agrément*, with 227 entries. At that time Griffons were judged in two weight classes, which were up to 3kg and 3-4.5 kg. At that time the Griffon Bruxellois could win a *Certificat de championnat*, but the Griffon Belge and Petit Brabançon were only awarded a *Prix d'honneur*. Belg Ch Loustic des Champs-Elysées and Daisy won the Certificates at that show.

The Warzée family bred Griffons with the affix du Clos des Orchidées for 50 years (1912-1962). Several Warzée ladies were enthusiastic breeders, but Mlle G Warzée was in the breed from 1921 until 1962. Her first Belgian Champion was Caline in 1926, a red mixed with black (*roux mélangé de noir*) rough bitch. She bred with the original Belgian lines and imported Mon Vieux, a red rough son of Eng Ch Felix of Irton, from France and Lalarookh Goblin, a red rough dog born in 1947, from Great Britain. These two are found in many of her pedigrees. Mlle Warzée bred 17 Belgian champions and had blacks and reds in both coats.

In 1962 Mme Nieuwland had her first litter with the affix de l'Enclos des Orchidées. Earlier she had several pet dogs. Her last litter was in 1973. She started with dogs from Mlle Warzée and continued breeding with these same lines. She imported from Italy Fiammetta di Montecavallo, a bitch also primarily based on the du Clos des Orchidées, and a granddaughter of the red rough bitch Ch Lalarookh Lindy from Great Britain. Mme Nieuwland bred nine Belgian champions and was the President of the Club du Griffon Bruxellois et du Chien de Dames. This club finished with her death: all Griffon items, books, pedigrees, pictures and club material were thrown away by her relatives. This was a great loss for the history of the breed in its country of origin.

Another lady, Mme Mahieu, acquired two Griffons in 1927 and campaigned the red rough dog Yser to Belgian champion. He was her first, last and only Belgian champion, although she bred 300 Griffons under the des Wallans affix from 1954 until 1984. I had the honour to meet this lady, but there was only one way to do that: you had to go to her home, because after the death of her husband she never left the walled property. I had to pass two fences before I was there, and only when she knew you were coming would she shut in her two Bouviers. Her Griffons, like the Bouviers, hardly ever saw strangers and used their teeth in a not-so-friendly way.

The heads of the dogs I saw were too extreme; their noses were very short, with a broad large nosepad, not between the eyes but above them. The eyes were almost too big. Some of them showed their tongues because there was no room in their mouths, because of the ultra-short faces. The coat texture was like the standard says: wired. They had true harsh wire coats and good colour, the type of coat we hardly see anymore in the Griffon world-wide. It's not a showy coat as one cannot really groom it. The size was good as far as I was concerned because I don't like the extremely small ones.

Mme Mahieu offered us a glass of wine. When the bottle was empty Juliette (the governess) was sent to the cellar for a new one. When Juliette was downstairs, Mme Mahieu went to the cellar door and shouted to her, 'Bring out a good one!' I suppose she decided that, as business had gone well, we could have a better bottle of wine.

On our second visit we brought a bitch named Madammeke to Mme Mahieu for a mating. The bitch was to stay for a week. During this period life became a little difficult in the kennel des Wallans: every time Juliette called our bitch, Madame Mahieu came or answered, because our bitch was also called Madame. Mme Mahieu died in 1988.

In the neighbourhood of Liège, we find the de la Verdière kennel belonging to M and Mme Graux-Maréchal. They live in a very nice old home with a big, old-fashioned orchard. Their kennel is internationally known for Boxers. In the early 1970s they took over all the Griffons from M and Mme Kuffer of Luxembourg. They started with the Dutch Heerschuur lines. In 1974 M and Mme Graux imported Starbeck Constans, a red rough dog by Starbeck Copper Dancer, and they took over a des Wallans bitch in 1988. So far they have bred two Belgian champions. They still breed Griffons in three colours and both coats.

In 1988 Mr Ketelslegers breathed new life in the old Griffon club, now teaming with another Belgian toy breed, the Papillon. The name was changed to Club Royal du Petit Griffon, du Brabançon et de l'Epagneul Nain Continental. He was President for several years and now he is Honorary President.

Mr Ketelslegers started to show the beautiful red smooth Multi Ch Little-Tipsy v Tschin-Tamani from Germany in 1988. She won BIS at the Dutch Griffon Club Show in 1991. He imported two more bitches from that kennel and three Starbeck and three Marquant Griffons from Great Britain, including Multi Ch Marquant Starbuster. From the United States he bought Multi Ch Treyacres Kipps Continued, a red rough bitch by the famous Am Ch Treyacres Zorro.

Mr Van Cauwenbergh of the Rahnee Dhao's affix imported Multi Ch Mike-Mar's of Rahnee Dhao's from the United States. He did a lot of winning with this dog, including the Toy Group at the World Dog Show in Germany 1991 and a BIS at the Belgian Club Show 1992. This red rough dog is the sire of two black-and-tan rough sons, Multi Chs Rahnee Dhao's Nikos and Nigger.

M de Meulenaer of the v d Havenstad affix, famous for breeding Miniature and Giant Schnauzers, bought Multi Ch Pamelot's Noble Antics in the United States. Noble Antics' daughter, the Dutch-bred Lycka Till Etoile, became the foundation bitch for this kennel. Bred to Multi Ch Alvermanneke v d Platte Belskes, she produced three World Winners; Royalqueen v d Havenstad (red rough), Ch Realangel (red rough) and her red smooth brother, Multi Ch Redrobin. These last two were the number one and two Best Toy in 1995 in Belgium. Redrobin was also the Top Griffon 1995 in Holland. With Multi Ch Windtrotter's Billy Boy, 'Etoile' produced another World Winner in 1996. This son, Sherif v d Havenstad, has now won the Toy Group twice in Belgium.

Mr Spruyt (du Paradis Noir) started with Multi Ch Little-Showgirl v Tschin-Tamani, a red rough bitch. He imported Starbeck Teresa, another red rough bitch, who won the Toy Group in Ghent 1995. Multi Ch Quentin du Paradis Noir, a red smooth dog belonging to Mr Deschuymere, won the Toy Group at Liège 1995.

The 'new' Belgian Griffon and Papillon Club organised its first CAC Show in 1994. The black-and-tan smooth bitch Belg Ch Lotje belonging to Mr den Otter and Mr Bleeker won BIS out of 62 Griffons.

Nowadays the Griffon gets a lot of attention at Belgian Championship Shows. Some Belgian judges have shown interest in the Griffon during the past few years, and now some even have a few Griffons of their own.

In Belgium it is not easy to get permission from the LOSH to interbreed the three varieties, Griffon Bruxellois, Griffon Belge and Petit Brabançon, which does not help the breed to progress. This is a pity: it would be good to see this tough little dog prosper in its country of origin.

Netherlands
Jan den Otter (v d Platte Belskes affix)

Ever since there have been Griffons Bruxellois in Belgium we have had something similar in the Netherlands. The Dutch Smoushond has the same roots as the Brussels Griffon (*smous* being the Dutch word for *griffon*) and the German Schnauzer. It was only in the Netherlands that the breed stayed as it was: a tough little working dog, looking like a mongrel. At one stage the Dutch Smoushond actually died out, but it is now being brought back under the supervision of Mrs Barkman v d Weel.

In 1890 a national stud book for dogs, *Nederlansch Honden Stam Boek* (NHSB), was started. At first it was only for gundogs and working dogs, but the first Griffons were entered in 1897 as follows:

No	Sex	Name	Sire	Dam
632	Dog	Quibus	Duc	Susea
633	Dog	Mercurius Marquis	Marquis	Mignon

In 1919 there was even a Griffon club, Club van Kleine Griffons en Brabançons. Since that time, there have always been a few Griffons in the Netherlands, but no line has survived from then to the present day.

In 1953 Miss Czopp of the v Siddhartha affix bred Josephine from two registered dogs (Sjors ex Dogi). At that time the register book was not closed and you could register a stray of the obvious Griffon type. After three generations with full pedigree sires had been entered in the register, the fourth generation appeared in the stud book with a normal pedigree. Miss Czopp imported many dogs from Belgium, one from France and a few, such as the black smooth Dutch Ch Starbeck Domata, from England. All these lines have now died out except for the founder bitch line (Dogi – Josephine – Petri v Siddhartha – Lily v d Zilversmidse – Guitje [a grey/blue smooth]). From Guitje came several more bitches who became brood bitches, with affixes such as v d Heerschuur, la Chielanka, v t'Strepto, and v Coranny. Miss Czopp stopped breeding in 1963.

In 1954 Miss Schaefer of the Tit Bit affix imported Skibbereen Tit Bit, a red rough bitch. A year later she also imported a red rough dog, Dutch/Int Ch Skibbereen Mark (Ch Skibbereen Victor of Campfield ex Skibbereen Candy). Mark was litter brother to Int Ch Skibbereen Felix, who went to Sweden. Miss Schaefer established her kennel from these two Griffons, using inbreeding, until 1966, when she imported Dutch/Int Ch Joriemour Hassan. She continued to breed until 1979, producing four champions under the Tit Bit affix. All Tit Bit dogs, except for one black-and-tan smooth, were red, rough and smooth.

In 1955 Mrs Phila Heerkens-Verschuuren (of the v d Heerschuur affix) was in England to buy a whippet. She saw a red smooth Griffon, and it was to become her first of many. Her mother had always kept a red smooth Griffon (Petit Brabançon) as a companion. Mrs Heerkens-Verschuuren, 80 years old and still full of energy, no longer breeds but is now an international judge. She is the doyenne of all Griffon people in the Netherlands and Belgium and, because of her great hospitality, she always has visitors. You will never find her door closed and she always

Dutch/Int/Swe/Belgian/German/VDH Ch Alvermanneke v d Platte Belskes. Photo: Hans Bleeker

has good advice, sought and unsought, for her visitors, like a true teacher (her original profession). She imported 15 Griffons, from the kennels Petworth, Tumpha, Shelvey, Gaystock and Crossgate in Great Britain. She also bought 10 more dogs from other Dutch breeders and used another 8 stud dogs not bred or imported by herself.

Stud dogs that had a great influence, not only in the v d Heerschuur kennels but on the breed as a whole in the Netherlands, were the black rough Shelvey Excello, his red rough son Dutch/Int Ch Kereltje v d Heerschuur and his red smooth son Orfeus v d Heerschuur. The red rough Crossgate Craxman was also often used. A totally new male line came with the black rough Nolleke v d Platte Belskes, who can be traced back to the old Belgian line of des Wallans from Mme Mahieu. This line goes back to de l'Enclos des Orchidées and du Clos des Orchidées.

In 40 years of breeding Mrs Heerkens-Verschuuren had only two black-and-tans. Altogether she bred 22 Dutch champions.

A few more kennels were started during the 1970s and 1980s, but all of them stopped after a few years. Mrs Siebelink-Tiekken started with two bitches from the Dogi line and bred five champions under her v Trixantia affix. Mrs Keizer v Dam, having also started with a bitch from the Dogi line, imported two red rough males, Gaystock Pollux of Mountwhistle and Gaystock le Taureau, and the red smooth bitch Dutch Ch Gaystock L'Ambroisie. She bred five champions under her affix v Coranny. Mrs v Veghel-v Maseland (affix v Doggersbank) imported the black rough Jerry (Ch Gay Cavalier of Kirkmarland ex Wylhylda's Bedelia) from Great Britain, and he gave several black-and-tans. In the 1980s the red smooth dog Dutch/Int/Lux Ch/World Winner '85 '86 Sjefke Jang Ketjil (combining Tit Bit and v d Heerschuur lines), bred and owned by Mr and Mrs v Schijen-v d Vliet, had some success.

At the end of the 1980s Mrs Heerkens-Lindeberg (second wife of Mr Heerkens) of the Pelasco kennel imported the red rough bitch Eloge of Cheerea from Finland and from Sweden the red rough dog Dutch/Int Ch Walliant's Knock Out and the red rough bitch Dutch/Int Ch Walliant's Illerim, a daughter of the first Swedish-bred BIS Griffon, Swe/Fin Ch Walliant's Ephraim. She bred the red smooth Dutch/Int/Belg/World Winner '89 Pelasco Casper out of these two Walliants. In total she has bred six champions.

A more recent kennel is that of Mrs Glaaser-Maher, who bred her first Beannachtai litter in 1991. This included the Top Winning Griffon 1993 in Dutch/Int/Ger/VDH/Lux Ch Beannachtai Arlon Ahain, a red rough (Multi Ch St Johns Sentimental Journey ex Peggy Sue v Duke's Paradise). In 1995 he won BIS at both the Belgian and the Dutch Griffon Club shows and his red rough sister from a repeat litter, Beannachtai Covergirl Chloé, owned by Miss v Schuppen, won the Toy Group at the Roosendaal International Championship Show. Chloé is the first Dutch-bred Griffon to win a Group in the Netherlands. In 1995 Mrs Glaaser imported the black rough male Jaydean Voyager from Great Britain.

The Platte Belskes kennel started in 1976 with the red smooth bitch Mafke v d Hesseldam from the Dogi line, though the actual breeding did not start until 1981. When mated to the black-and-tan rough Fidel Castro v Doggerbank she produced several black-and-tans, among them top Dutch winning black-and-tan Dutch/Int/Lux Ch Prulleke v d Platte Belskes (bitch). She won in Amsterdam, Brussels and Luxembourg when the Griffon Bruxellois and Griffon Belge were still judged together and in Paris/Pontoise at the age of seven.

A daughter of British import Crossgate Calyx, the red smooth Dutch/Int/Lux Ch Tutje v d Heerschuur produced the best female offspring in the 1980s, including four Dutch champions.

Through the years, Mr den Otter and Mr Bleeker imported 10 dogs from kennels all over the world, such as Starbeck (Great Britain), St Johns (United States)

Dutch/Int Ch Sam I Am of St John. Photo: Hans Bleeker

Dutch/Int/Belgian/German/VDH Ch Romuluske v d Platte Belskes. Photo: Hans Bleeker

and other European countries. Their Belgian red rough import, Dutch/Int/Am Ch Jakke-Plat-Belske Babette's Pride, of Danish and English stock, was widely used at stud in Holland. He later went to the United States.

In the late 1980s/early 1990s Dutch/Int Ch Starbeck Centime was the Top Winning Bitch. She was BIS at the Dutch Griffon Club Show 1992.

In 1991 they imported red rough Dutch/Int/Belg/Am Ch St Johns Sentimental Journey, a red rough dog by Am Ch Treyacres U Asked For It (a red smooth son of Eng/Am Ch Beauview Bona Fide) out of Am Ch Kelim's Bottoms Up, bred by Mr and Mrs Bazell from Ohio. He was Top Griffon in 1991, Top Stud 1993, 1994 and 1995, and he is the sire of 12 champions all over the world. His son, Dutch/Int/Swedish/Belg/Ger/VDH Ch/World Winner 94 Alvermanneke v d Platte Belskes (ex Starbeck Centime) was the top-winning Griffon 1994 in Germany, Belgium and the Netherlands. Alvermanneke was BIS at the Toy Championship Show at Haan-Gruiten, Germany, and at the Dutch Griffon Club Show 1994. His half-brother, Dutch/Int/Swe/Lux Ch Voila-ke v d Platte Belskes, owned by Mrs Hedfors, was the top-winning smooth of 1994 in Sweden. He produced black-and-tans in Norway, Sweden and the Netherlands. The black rough dog Romuluske v d Platte Belskes by Dutch/Int/Finnish Ch Starbeck Sinful Secret is the top-winning black rough so far in the breed. He won the following championship titles: Dutch, International, Belgian, German, VDH, FCI-European Ch '92, World Winner '94 '95. He has also won a Group and several Group placings during his four-year show career. The influence of some other St Johns lines is very high in this kennel.

In 1992 Mr den Otter and Mr Bleeker published the *Dutch Champion Book 1901-1992* and in 1995 to mark the occasion of the 100th Expo St Hubert (the World Dog Show 1995 held in Brussels) the *Belgian Champion Book 1892-1994*. At the Amsterdam Winners Championship Show in 1993 they had three BOBs (Bruxellois, Belge & Brabançon), a unique event in the breed. In 1995 the affix Leo Belgicus was established to continue the successful story of v d Platte Belskes, which has bred and/or owned 25 Champions, of which 15 have the v d Platte Belskes affix.

The only BIS Griffon we had in Holland at an all-breeds show (Zuidlaren 1987) was the Swedish-bred rough red dog Multi Ch Amarillo, owned by Mrs Weiglin of Denmark. He is by Ch Starbeck Czigany ex Walliants Yaquelle (a granddaughter of Ch Chilka Kelly of Mahnyar).

In 1990 the Club van Kleine Griffons en Brabandertjes, founded in 1977, organised its fourth Championship Club Show. At that time we needed 30 Griffons Bruxellois, 30 Griffons Belge and 30 Petits Brabançons entered at this show to get Champion status from the Raad van Beheer op Kynologisch Gebied in Nederland (Dutch Kennel Club). It was the largest Griffon gathering ever held on the Continent of Europe, with 126 dogs. Miss Gaines of the English kennel Gaystock and Mr Prins were our two judges. The American-bred Multi Ch Windtrotter's Al Jolson, owned by Mrs Koskelin of Finland, became BIS.

In 1986 Mr Bleeker introduced the American way of preparing the coat of the Griffon to the Netherlands. A neat coat on the body and head and more furnishings on the legs gives the rough Griffon the impression of the Belgian draught-horse. Before that Griffons were shown in a stripped coat, and some still are. Since then, Griffons have been seen in the Ring of Honour, winning several Group placings. Mr Bazell explained why the Griffon has to have the wonderful beard and leg furnishings. The Griffon is a stable dog which takes care of vermin, such as rats. The beard and luxuriant hair on the legs afford the Griffon some protection against rat bites.

The Griffon population is very small in the Netherlands. Over the last 25 years we had an average of 48 registered puppies a year. In 1990 we started to judge the Griffon Bruxellois by FCI rules, separating the Griffon Bruxellois (red rough) from the Griffon Belge (roughs in black, black-and-tan and black with red hairs mixed). The Petit Brabançons (smooths) have always been judged separately from the roughs. I doubt if the breed benefits from this as it means that the three varieties are breeds in their own right. We can only interbreed them with a permission preceding any mating. Normally the Raad van Beheer agrees with every application to interbreed.

Germany
Jan den Otter (v d Platte Belskes affix)

In Germany a few breeders started and stopped. Mrs Charlier (formerly Niedzwetzki) of the kennel v Tschin-Tamani started with two red smooth daughters out of the red smooth Ger Ch Dozmare Dorothea Rose, a sister to Ch Dozmare Damask Rose, by Multi Ch El Jalisco's Tarkas bred by Mr Dickmann.

Breeder Jan den Otter with Dutch/Int/Belgian Ch Voici-ke v d Platte Belskes. Photo: Karl Donvil

'Tarkas' is by Int/German Ch Dozmare Demon King, a son of Eng Ch Ardtighe Edouard. Mrs Charlier bought Multi Ch Jasper Babette's Pride, brother to Ch Jakke-Plat-Belske Babette's Pride, in Belgium and took two matings from Multi Ch Amarillo. In the 1980s and early 1990s hers was one of the most important kennels in Europe and produced several outstanding dogs, including four World Winners. Her top-winning Griffon is Multi Ch Little-Quando v Tschin-Tamani, a red smooth dog. Unfortually she no longer breeds because of pressure of work.

Mr Henseler (Red Hot Hottentot's) was very successful with Quando's brother, Multi Ch Little-Questor v Tschin-Tamani. This red smooth dog won BIS at the Toy Championship Show at Rüsselsheim 1988 in Germany, most unusual for a smooth. Mr Henseler later bought a bitch from Tschin-Tamani and three bitches from Huvikummun (Finland). His F-litter by Dutch/Int Ch Starbeck Crimson ex Ger Ch Huvikummun Happy Jane I Am produced two World Winners '94; the red smooth Multi Ch Red Hot Hottentot's Fatal Attraction and her red rough sister Multi Ch Red Hot Hottentot's Faye Dunaway. Both are campaigned by the Dutch kennel Leo Belgicus.

Mr Heim imported three Griffons from Great Britain in the late 1980s and early 1990s: black rough bitch Ger/Aus Ch Chosendale Cherelle, black-and-tan rough bitch Multi Ch Chosendale Calenduca and black rough dog Ger Ch Fennymore Pistols At Dawn. He never could find the time to produce a litter with these three champions.

In Germany the Griffon is represented by the Verbandes Deutscher Kleinhundezüchter e v, a breed club for Toy dogs. The distance between the breeders in Germany and the Kleinhunde organisation is very short. The Kleinhunde Club is a organization within the VDH (German KC) and has the right to make its own official pedigrees and rules for breeding. They see our breed as one and name it Zwerggriffon, but the three varieties are still judged the same way as in the other FCI-member countries.

Austria
Jan den Otter (v d Platte Belskes affix)

In Austria Mrs Garhofer (Ilkey Moor) imported from Great Britain the red rough dog Gaystock Force Majeur and Ch Cynjon Asset Abound, a red rough bitch. Her two red smooths, Ch Ilkey Moor Wee Imp and Ch Ilkey Moor Kiss 'N Tell, both became World Winners in Vienna 1996.

The Czech Republic and Slovakia
Jan den Otter (v d Platte Belskes affix)

Mr Penicka (Kompas Rose) started as the first Griffon breeder in Eastern Europe in the beginning of the 1980s, after having bred Boxers and French Bulldogs, with Heerschuur stock. After some colour problems he needed a complete new male line and imported Int/CS Ch Grolleke K Rose v d Platte Belskes, a red smooth dog (Ch Eli-Jalisco's Tarkas ex Willowbrooks Plat Bels Anje). 'Anje' is by Ch Beauview Bona Fide. He took a mating from Ch St Johns Sentimental Journey and bought a red rough bitch, Valiske v d Platte Belskes, in the early 1990s. From Sweden he imported the black-and-tan smooth bitch Ratcatcher's Electra and has bred (so far) two black-and-tans. His black smooth bitch Czigany Kompas Rose produced two World Winners; the black rough Ch Romuluske v d Platte Belskes and Ch Fee-Black Kompas Rose. The latter won his title in Vienna 1996. Because of his energy they also have their own Griffon Club.

Hungary
Jan den Otter (v d Platte Belskes affix)

Mrs Tarjan (Red Devils) is the first Griffon breeder and judge in Hungary. From Austria she imported Ilkey Moor Captain Hook, from Finland a Huvikummun bitch and from Holland a Pelasco bitch, all red rough. Mrs Tarjan recently imported Starbeck Rosenkavalier, a red rough dog out of Eng Ch Starbeck Crystal Song, from Great Britain. Her red smooth bitch Red Devils Gene became World Winner 1995.

Dutch/Int Ch Erasmuske v d Platte Belskes. Photo: Hans Bleeker

General Health

Abnormal puppies

Occasionally puppies are born either not complete or with an abnormal function such as a cleft palate. As soon as a puppy is known to have an abnormality it should quietly be taken from its dam and, sad though it may be, it should be painlessly destroyed.

Abscesses

An abscess can form almost anywhere on a dog. The kind you are most likely to encounter is caused by the duct of the anal sac becoming blocked by septic matter. In the early stages of the blockage the dog will appear uncomfortable and may try to lick himself or drag his hindquarters in an attempt to relieve the discomfort. As time goes by the area around the anus becomes very swollen and tender because of the formation of the abscess. Care of the dog's anal glands as described in Chapter Four will prevent the trouble. In the event of an abscess forming veterinary treatment is necessary as soon as it is discovered.

Accidents

After an accident either in the home or on the road a dog should be handled very carefully to avoid doing more damage. Also, the owner should avoid being bitten by a frightened dog, because a dog in shock may not know what it is doing.

Veterinary aid is required immediately to assess the damage and treat the dog. The recovery powers of a dog are astonishing, so a distraught owner may find his or her pet fully recovered in a short space of time. However, sadly there are always a few fatalities as a result of accidents.

Anorexia

When a normally healthy dog refuses his food and there is no apparent reason, such as fever or something stuck in his teeth that prevents chewing, the dog could be suffering from anorexia and veterinary advice is necessary. A dog can become very thin indeed as the stomach shrinks through lack of nourishment. Apart from following veterinary advice, a dessertspoonful of Complan mixed with a little water once or twice a day can be helpful during the treatment period.

Arthritis and rheumatism

Both these conditions are associated with the older dog. In severe cases your veterinary surgeon will recommend pain-relieving tablets. Mild attacks usually right themselves when the weather is less damp and with sensible general care and consideration.

Bad breath

Bad breath is usually due to bad teeth and not often associated with Griffons: as a breed they are well-known for their good teeth. A possible exception can be treated with Amplex tablets or as advised by your vet.

Balantis

Balantis is an infection of the sheath of the penis, quite common in young males. The symptom is a thick, white discharge that usually clears up with extra hygienic care and frequent bathing to keep the dog fresh. If it persists, consult your vet.

Bites

If your dog is bitten by another dog, take your dog to your vet for treatment in case the wound becomes septic. Similarly, an owner bitten by a dog should consult their doctor at once in case of infection.

Bladder stones and cystitis

Bladder stones give the same symptoms as cystitis; a frequent desire to urinate, the urine sometimes becoming blood-stained and the act of urinating being painful. Urgent veterinary advice is needed to alleviate the discomfort of cystitis and an operation may be necessary for the treatment of bladder stones.

Blindness

Due to their excellent sense of sound and smell most dogs who lose their sight in old age can manage quite easily in familiar surroundings such as their home and garden without too many problems.

Burns and scalds

Keep the dog quiet, apply cold water to the affected part and call your vet immediately.

Cancer

Not all growths are dangerous; some tumours may be benign. In the older dog, harmless fatty growths may appear. Whatever the symptom, veterinary advice should be sought promptly for a correct diagnosis and treatment if necessary.

Canine hepatitis

see **Inoculation**

Canker

The symptoms of ear canker, or otitis as it is clinically called, are a dog scratching its ears or shaking its head. Examination of the ear will reveal brownish matter in the cavity. In a mild case, the ear can be wiped out carefully with an antiseptic Pet

Dog Wipe and a little branded ear canker lotion can be applied to the ear. If the ears are red and swollen and have an offensive smell they need urgent veterinary attention and should not on any account be touched by the amateur.

Collapse

Griffons very occasionally collapse with heat stroke. It is a dangerous condition requiring urgent attention from a vet. Before help arrives try to keep the animal as cool as possible. If it should happen at a show, a vet is always present and he will give your do immediate treatment. I have only seen two dogs with heat stroke, both at Championship shows; it is a frightening experience for dog and owner.

Collapse from a heart attack is a different problem: the dog needs to be kept warm and quiet and usually comes to quite quickly. However, veterinary advice is still necessary and the vet will probably seek to prevent further attacks by prescribing heart tablets to stabilise the condition.

Diarrhoea

Diarrhoea can be a symptom of many illnesses and should always be taken seriously because, with a small dog, dehydration can set in very quickly. If the diarrhoea is caused by something you know may have upset the dog an invalid type diet with no meat for 24 hours should clear up the problem. Anything more serious requires veterinary advice.

Distemper

see Inoculation

You can help to make sure these healthy 10-week-old sisters remain well by having them inoculated.
Photo: Hans Bleeker

Eclampsia or milk fever

Eclampsia is described in Chapter Six and urgently requires treatment by a vet.

Entropion

Entropion is an inherited condition affecting the dog's eye-lids that makes one or both lids turn slightly inwards, causing irritation and weeping from the eye. The cure is a small operation. This clears up the trouble but an animal with this condition should not be used for breeding. As far as I know it is not a condition from which Griffons suffer.

Eye problems

The eyes of the Griffon Bruxellois are large and therefore a little more susceptible to possible damage. Wiping out with damp cotton wool and making sure that the hair is trimmed away from the eyes is usually an effective remedy.

For any serious infection, such as a heavy discharge or an eye ulcer, seek veterinary advice as soon as possible to prevent permanent damage to the sight.

False pregnancy

Some females, although unmated during a season, show signs of pregnancy and their teats swell visibly. It resolves itself when the imagined pregnancy comes to an end. However, if you have any problems or cannot exhibit your female, seek veterinary advice.

Fractures

Keep the dog as quiet and immobile as possible and telephone your vet for help.

Hard Pad

see **Inoculation**

Hernia, umbilical

Umbilical hernias are not uncommon in Griffons. They are small swellings of the umbilicus where the abdominal wall has not quite closed and do not usually cause any problems.

Hernia, inguinal

In females these hernias can occur either side of the lower stomach area, the groin. It would be most unwise to attempt breeding from such a female until it is safely repaired by an operation. Even then, breeding should only be allowed after consultation with your vet.

Inoculation

Distemper, hard pad (a variation of distemper), canine hepatitis, leptospirosis and parvovirus are controlled by inoculation during puppyhood. Vaccinations against distemper, hepatitis and leptospirosis are particluarly effective.

It must be remembered that older dogs can contact distemper with fatal results, so regular boosters should not be ignored on the grounds that adult dogs are not susceptible to this disease.

There has been enormous progress in the prevention of parvovirus and, although there are rare strains of the disease that are not prevented by vaccination, owners should in no way be deterred from having their puppies fully protected to lessen the results of any possible infection.

Kennel cough

Kennel cough does not usually apply if the dogs are mostly confined to the house, but any unusual cough requires advice. Preventive vaccinations are available which minimise the effects of this ailment. You should certainly consider vaccination if your dog is to spend any time in boarding kennels.

Lameness

Check for the more usual causes, such as a thorn in the foot, a cut pad, or nettle stings, which can drive a dog frantic. If there is no obvious reason for the lameness it is best to consult your vet.

Leptospirosis

see **Inoculation**

Mastitis

Mastitis is an infection of the mammary glands, which become swollen and require urgent professional treatment.

Metritis

This is an abnormal discharge from the uterus, usually affecting a newly-whelped female, and again requires urgent veterinary help.

Parvovirus

see **Inoculation**

Patella luxation

Patella luxation is a malformation or injury of the stifle joint. This is perhaps better described as the equivalent to the knee joint of a human but situated on the hind leg of a dog. The patella is similar to a knee cap, which can slip out of the knee joint. On a dog it slips out of the groove designed for it in the thighbone.

Patella luxation can be seen on affected dogs by their manner of walking when the joint slips in and out, causing the dog to drop or favour the leg to a greater or lesser extent. If the luxation is slight, it is barely noticeable and does not appear to worry the dog - some even get by in the show ring. In bad cases the dog is obviously uncomfortable and the owner has the choice of giving the dog a very quiet life, an operation if a vet considers it likely to be successful, or sadly having the dog painlessly put to sleep.

Poison

If you think your dog has eaten poison it is vital to contact your vet without delay.

Pyometra

A pyometra can occur in a young female but is usually associated with the older female. Some of the symptoms are: a distended stomach, sickness (of solids and even water), discharge from the vulva, and a marked thirst. The condition requires

A picture of health: Cleevecloud Czarina

urgent veterinary attention; otherwise the female will die as a result of an accumulation of pus in the uterus.

Sexual maturity

When fully mature a dog should have two testicles descended into the scrotum. Toy breeds can be much later reaching maturity than large breeds.

From information I have gathered, Toys and other small breeds, such as Bostons, can take up to 18 months to develop. In one case, a Griffon became sexually mature at 10 years of age! Normally one likes to see a puppy fully developed by four months old, although some may take a few months longer.

In the very early days of showing Griffons in Britain the judges would comment in their critiques of dogs only having one descended testicle. This was many years before the banning by The Kennel Club of dogs exhibited at shows without two fully descended testicles. A dog with only one is known as a *monorchid* and is capable of siring litters, although some of the male puppies may inherit the same condition. When neither testicle has descended the dog is known as a *cryptorchid* and is incapable of reproduction.

It is worth remembering that dogs exported to some foreign countries require a certificate of entirety on the part of the sire of the dog to be exported.

Skin diseases

All skin problems, whatever their cause, need veterinary advice to ensure that the correct treatment is effected.

Snorts

New Griffon owners are sometimes concerned by the way their dog may occasionally cough or breath heavily in a distressed manner, its flanks heaving; it could be described as a snort. Snorts are common to many small dogs, not only those with short faces, and are nothing to worry about. Some dogs snort occasionally, some not at all. If it does happen, put your thumb over the dog's nose: the dog gasps and all is well again.

Teeth

Some puppies retain their baby teeth longer than they should, and their second teeth appear before they have lost all the milk teeth, crowding the mouth and causing discomfort. An affected puppy holds its mouth incorrectly, almost appearing to have a wry mouth. The treatment is a comparatively small operation to remove the offending teeth. Sympathetic handling and care after the operation will ensure that the puppy does not react badly to any later examination.

From an exhibitor's point of view, it is desirable to see level incisors between the canine teeth of a well undershot mouth. It is quite normal, however, to find that there are only four teeth because the mouth is not capacious enough to accommodate more teeth. Provided the mouth appears broad and does not look narrow and pinched it is not too grave a fault. In many small breeds a judge is not expected to examine the teeth; in Griffons it is usual only to check the mouth shape.

Toes – interdigital cysts

Interdigital cysts between the toes are very painful and can best be avoided by keeping the hair under the feet short and free from mud and grit. If a dog is licking its foot and has a swelling there, it requires treatment from your vet.

Tonsillitis

Tonsillitis is fairly common in dogs. The glands at each side of the throat become swollen and the dog will cough, appear very unhappy and run a temperature. Consult your vet: he or she will probably prescribe antibiotics, which will provide quick relief for the dog and cure the problem

Webbed feet

There used to be a percentage of Griffons with what was termed *webbed feet*. This was not a true webbing, but a joining of the two centre toes on the front feet and sometimes the two centre hind toes. This so-called abnormality was greatly frowned on by the Belgians who decided to eradicate it altogether and, by doing so, lost the greater proportion of their breeding stock. In Britain webbing was not made a Kennel Club disqualification and over the years has never caused any problems. Two very famous past champions who had webbed feet were Ch Skibbereen Beau Brummel and Ch Skibbereen Victor of Campfield, both beautiful dogs who left behind them many champions that feature prominently in the pedigrees of today's champions. Hand-in-hand with webbed feet went the very best heads that could be seen on Griffons, greatly prized by serious breeders.

Strangely enough, the old breed of Pyrame, now extinct, was a rough-coated black-and-tan dog with webbed feet. The Pyrame was used in the development of the King Charles Spaniel and it would not be unnatural to wonder if there was any possible connection between the Pyrame and the Griffon Bruxellois. King Charles Spaniels also sometimes have webbed feet, often associated with a stronger head.

Worms

After puppy worming, dogs should be wormed regularly once a year with a proprietary brand or as advised by your vet. Should you suspect that worms are affecting your dog, obtain professional advice.

Conclusion

Finally, to anyone who buys a Griffon puppy or, for that matter, an adult dog: you have chosen a breed unlike any other. They make up in character and intelligence for any loss of size compared to the larger breeds of dog. The Griffon will unobtrusively take over your home and your heart.

The Griffon Today

In Britain today, there are three thriving Breed Clubs and a Breeders Association.

The Griffon Bruxellois Club

The Griffon Bruxellois Club is by far the oldest and will celebrate its centenary in 1997. During the 1980s its secretary was Mrs Patricia Wiggins, a well-known breeder and exhibitor.

The new Chairman of the Club is Mr Eike Herold with the Bentwood affix. Mr Herold, formerly a breeder of Pugs, came into Griffons a good many years ago. The current President is Mrs Cythia Howard of the Cynjon Griffons. The immediate past President is Mrs Phylis Woolford with her Krandon blacks and, before that, Miss Betty Gorringe, of the Litahni affix, who has specialised in smooth red Griffons since the early 1940s. Miss Maria Oliver holds the busy post of Secretary and combines it with the Editorship of the quarterly magazine, *Griffon Bruxellois Bulletin*. This magazine, first published in 1954, is of great historical interest. Miss Oliver also runs a small kennel of Birchend Griffons. Mrs Pamela Sturman, the archivist, still compiles all archives relating to the Griffon Bruxellois.

The club puts on two shows and a garden party each year and a club symposium every two years.

The Northern Griffon Bruxellois Club

In the North of England, there is the Northern Griffon Bruxellois Club. During the 1980s the secretary was Miss Ursula Gregory, a young-at-heart senior citizen with a lifetime enthusiasm for Griffondom. Miss Gregory, with her Committee, ran a lively Club that made all southern Griffon exhibitors who managed to travel up to the northern shows very welcome. On retiring as secretary after 25 years of service in this post she became President.

Sadly, Miss Gregory died in the Spring of 1990. Her well-known dogs carried the affix Gregtoi. The affix was shared with her sisters, particularly Esther who was the most involved. They

A greetings card produced by The Griffon Bruxellois Club.

had bred Pekingese before Griffons and for a while continued in both breeds before settling entirely with Griffons.

Miss Ursula Gregory was succeeded by Mrs Norma Wiley, who recently retired to give more time to her dogs. Mrs Wiley is a more recent Griffon breeder who shares the Harland affix with her husband, David. They breed Cavalier King Charles, Griffon Bruxellois and I believe still have a soft spot for Collies. Mrs Wiley has written by hand a most concise documentation of all British Griffon champions. These booklets are well worth obtaining for historical reference and, if I may say so, her exceptional script makes it all the more worthwhile.

The next Secretary of the club was Mrs June Burke, who bred the lovely Ch Markath Harbour Light, made up in 1978. She was followed by the current Secretary, Mrs Brenda Roberts.

Until recently, the Northern Griffon Bruxellois Club had no publication of its own. The 'Northern Notes' were published in *The Griffon Bruxellois Bulletin*. In June 1990 the first solo *Northern Newsletter* was published, ably edited by Mrs Maureen Higgins. Maureen is also the 'Breed Notes' writer for *Our Dogs*. Perhaps one day in the future there will emerge a *Northern Newsletter Magazine*.

The Griffon Bruxellois Club of Scotland

In Scotland there is a small but active Griffon Club, whose current Secretary is Mrs Charlotte. Previously it was ably led by Mrs Jean Dorward (Secretary) and her husband Mr David Dorward (Chairman). Despite distances, Mr and Mrs Dorward attend many shows with their Dajela Griffons.

The President of the Griffon Bruxellois Club of Scotland is Mrs Jean Connor who made up the first Scottish Griffon dog champion in her home-bred Inchlee Fireflash in 1990.

The Griffon Bruxellois Breeders Association

There is also the Griffon Bruxellois Breeders Association, formed in 1982 and designed for the benefit of breeders and pet owners alike. This association also runs shows and holds seminars and judging assessments. A quarterly magazine, *Progress*, is also published.

The Griffon Bruxellois Breeders Association has seen changes in administration in the late 1980s following the sudden death of its Chairman, Mr Michael Payne MRCVS. Mr Paul Stannard, a well known judge and breeder of Pekingese and Griffons, was elected Chairman. Mr Stannard's wife Mrs Elizabeth Stannard also shows the more recently imported Bolognese. Together they exhibit under the Sharita affix.

Mrs Peggy Searl, who guided the Association through its early years and Kennel Club recognition, retired as Secretary in 1988, to give more time to herself, her garden and her varied judging commitments. Since then, the Secretary has been Mr Peter Watkins, who is now running an ever-expanding Association of breeders and pet owners, who join together at various social and educational meetings. Mr Watkins, a successful breeder and exhibitor, holds the Bembridge affix and is a judge of Cavalier King Charles and Griffons.

Mrs Cynthia Howard, who designed the original format and edited *Progress* so well, resigned through pressure of a full-time career in 1989. However, Mrs Howard still breeds and shows Griffons with her Cynjon affix and is a judge of Griffons and President of the Griffon Bruxellois Club. Mrs Lucille Dangerfield, who needs no introduction, took over the editorship until 1992, since when the editor has been Mrs Pat Crick, who has continued to update the magazine in quality and content in her own able and amusing fashion.

Ch Skibbereen Victor of Campfield. Photo: Thomas Fall

Mrs Eileen Street

Mrs Eileen Street owned the world-famous kennel of Skibbereen Griffons and was the foremost authority and a specialist Griffon judge both home and overseas. Through the years Mrs Street made up a record 32 champions, making her name and affix synonymous with Griffons. Her most renowned champion was Ch Skibbereen Victor of Campfield who, after the Second World War, when the breed of Griffon Bruxellois was in the doldrums, had the distinction of becoming the first-ever Griffon to be BIS at a general Championship Show. On his retirement, unbeaten at five, he had notched up two BISs at general Championship Shows along with 21 CCs and 21 BISs at non-Championship Shows.

On her retirement from showing, Mrs Street continued to judge and took great interest in all that was going on in the Griffon world. She became Vice-President of the Griffon Bruxellois Club and Patron of the Griffon Bruxellois Breeders Association.

The Griffon world mourned Eileen's sudden death in November 1990.

Stanley Dangerfield

Anyone with an interest in dogs and a television set will know of Stanley Dangerfield. As a well-known author, journalist and all-round international Championship Show judge, he did much to promote Griffons to the general public. His television programme *The Good Companions* ran for five years during the 1950s and featured Mr Dangerfield's little Griffon, Tazzie. In the 1980s Mr Dangerfield regularly

Ch Chosendale Seamus, only black-and-tan smooth champion.

broadcast from Crufts Dog Show each year and was the show's Chief Steward. He judged dogs in some 30 different countries, which must be a record. With his wife Lucille he owned the black-and-tan smooth Ch Chosendale Seamus, who gained 15 CCs, and his son, a little black smooth. For many years he was President of the Griffon Bruxellois Club.

Sadly, Mr Dangerfield died in 1988. His wife, Mrs Lucille Dangerfield, carries on the interest in Griffons by judging.

Other breeders and dogs

Many owners of well-known affixes whose names can be found on the pedigrees of dogs shown in Britain and abroad during the 1970s and 1980s have retired from active participation in breeding and showing Griffons. The combined incidence of retirement and loss of elderly exhibitors has been reflected in the show ring by

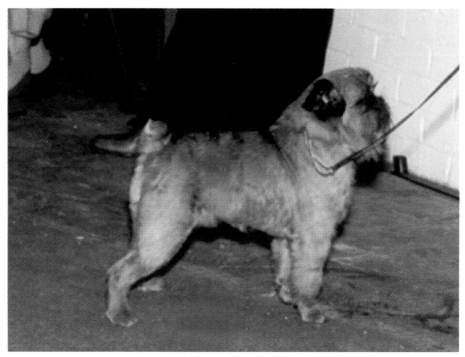

Ch Gaystock L'Incroyable.

Miss Anne Tyler with friend.

smaller classes, particularly amongst the senior dogs. However, this has only been a phase in the story of Griffons. Now there is an upsurge of young and not-so-young new exhibitors, all making a welcome challenge in the show ring and beginning to establish themselves as the breeder/exhibitor of tomorrow.

The most outstanding Griffon Bruxellois exhibited in the 1970s was undoubtedly the red rough Ch Hunters Melody of Gregtoi, bred by the Misses Gregory but owned and exhibited by Mr Howard Ogden. Hunters Melody was a joy to watch in the show ring for his soundness and outgoing temperament, which in his career earned him 30 CCs.

Two large and most successful kennels are the Starbecks and Gaystocks. Mrs Ann Fenn, with her Starbeck affix, runs a highly successful kennel: her dogs are acknowledged world-wide as a result of her many exports across the globe. At

Ch Mahnyar Dragonfly, all-time top-winning black-and-tan bitch. Photo: Christina Lees

home Mrs Fenn has bred and made up 13 champions in 10 years. Her many awards include the honour of BIS at a general Championship Show at Manchester 1982.

Mrs Deborah Gaines and her partner, daughter Miss Tessa Gaines, ran a consistently successful kennel for a great many years with the Gaystock affix and have a string of championships behind them and successful exports to the United States, Scandinavia and Australia. Sadly Mrs Gaines died in 1983 but the kennel continues with Miss Gaines at the helm.

Mr Jack Ellithorn with his well-known Glenrig affix, having retired from breeding dogs, sadly died in the spring of 1997. His skill as a specialist judge will be greatly missed.

Mr Keith Langston, who retired very early in life from breeding his Keitoy Griffons, still finds time to judge the breed. Mr Langston is a very interesting man to watch in the ring: his manner of judging is unique.

Mrs Molly Dixon holds the Otterbourne affix. Miss Betty Thomas holds the Gerrards affix, which was also held by her mother. Mrs Enders has the Utopian affix. Mrs Gwen Davitt holds the Tumfa affix. Mrs Phoebe Cuming has the Polrose affix. Miss April Proctor with the Tzigane affix had her name in the Crufts Roll of Honour when she was BIS at Crufts in 1955 with a Standard Poodle.

Today, most Griffon kennels belong to small breeder/exhibitors, some of whose affixes are no less well-known although they may have fewer puppies available. A list of some Griffon affixes will be found at Appendix B.

Griffon personalities in recent years

During the intervening years several well-known personalities associated with Griffons have sadly left us.

Mr Michael Payne MRCVS, Chairman of the Griffon Bruxellois Breeders Association and a former Chairman of the Griffon Bruxellois Club, died in 1986. Mr Payne's Griffon affix was Rathensis, shared and continued by his wife, Mrs Pamela Payne, now President of the Association.

Miss E M Sautelle Barter died in 1989. She was a Griffon breeder of many years standing with her famous Barratelle affix. It would probably be fair to say that her main love was the red smooth Griffon. Among her champions was Ch Barratelle Red Tarzan, whose head is portrayed in the standard of the Griffon clubs' handbooks. Miss Barter was a past President of the Griffon Bruxellois Club. Her other interests included the theatre (Miss Barter's sister is an actress) and horse racing.

Formally, Miss Barter shared a house in Worcestershire with Miss Muriel Forwood of the equally well-known affix Enavant. Miss Forwood died two weeks after a car accident, when returning from a show in 1972. Miss Forwood was also greatly interested in the theatre and at the time of her death was Senior Governor of the Royal Shakespeare Theatre, Stratford-on-Avon. Miss Forwood was for many years President of the Northern Griffon Bruxellois Club and she was the first Editor in 1954 of the *Griffon Bruxellois Bulletin*.

Many more breeder/exhibitors have cut back or retired from breeding dogs. Nevertheless, much to the benefit of the Griffon Bruxellois, several of the former exhibitors continue to judge and lecture.

Mrs Pat Wiggins, former Secretary and Chairman of the Griffon Bruxellois Club, has to some extent curtailed her Griffon breeding programme. However, she continues to give her services as a specialist judge of Griffons. Mrs Wiggins showed her dogs under the Andiron affix.

Mrs Marjorie Clark of the Joriemour affix announced her retirement from judging Griffons after she adjudicated at Richmond Championship Show in 1989. Happily, she continues as a very active President of the Griffon Bruxellois Breeders Association, attends all the meetings and is always willing to give advice from her wealth of knowledge and experience in several breeds of dog. Mrs Clarke, now almost 90 years old, is a most respected member and has been Patron of the Association since 1991.

Mrs Phyllis Bird (Incatan), affectionately known by her friends as Birdie, died in 1992, as did Mrs Dovey Kirk. Both were prominent members of the Griffon Bruxellois Club and the Griffon Bruxellois Breeders Association, and they will be remembered affectionately by the members of these organisations. In that year we also lost Mrs Ena Basset who, although she was perhaps better known for Dachshunds, bred and judged Griffons for many years.

Miss Raphine Deck was a prominent member of the Griffon Bruxellois Club and served as its Secretary for 12 years. With her Tunlake affix she specialised in breeding black-and-tans. I would think there is Tunlake breeding behind the majority of today's black-and-tan Griffons. Miss Deck retired for health reasons and died in 1993. Over the years Miss Deck and Miss Ann Tyler (Shelvey Griffons) together compiled *Lines and Families*, originated by Miss Marjorie Cousins.

Mr Desmond Gregory, a past *Griffon Bruxellois Bulletin* Editor, Secretary for 12 years and finally Chairman of the Griffon Bruxellois Club, eventually retired from the show ring shortly before his death in 1995. His successful affix Chosendale carried on through the occasional litter he bred for other people to show, but the breeding of birds became his main area of interest. He had large aviaries of Border Canaries and Parakeets, which he used to show during their short exhibition period each year. However, Mr Gregory did not forsake the dog show ring altogether, but continued to judge and lecture on the subject of Griffons right up to the end.

Despite these and other farewells, the present day top kennels, large and sometimes very small, carry on their successful way. Counteracting all the departures, many new breeders have fallen under the spell of Griffons and are coming into the ring to enjoy their first triumphs. It would be nice to see again the instantly recognisable lines of individual breeders, which to some extent seems to be missing at the moment. Perhaps this particular situation will improve as all the many new breeders become more established in future years.

Perhaps in the 1990s it is also time to look at the future of our breed. We Griffon breeders may sometimes dream of breeding the perfect Griffon. It is a praiseworthy enough thought; we can all dream of improving our dogs. However, let us hope we do not interpret *improve* as *change*. In some breeds, change has not necessarily brought improvement. Let us Griffon breeders keep in mind dogs such as Ch Skibbereen Victor of Campfield (page 118), vintage 1950, as we go forward into the next century!

A head study of Ch Harland Ratiffany. Photo: Martin Leigh

The Breed Standard

Ch Starbeck Crystal Rainbow, record Toy Group and BIS All-Breed winner. Photo: David Dalton

The Kennel Club Breed Standard - Griffon Bruxellois
By kind permission of The Kennel Club

General Appearance A cobby, well-balanced, square little dog, giving appearance of measuring the same from withers to tail as from withers to ground.

Characteristics Smart little dog with disposition of a terrier. Two varieties, rough coated, Griffon Bruxellois and smooth coated, Petit Brabançon. Both with pert, monkey-like expression, heavy for size.

Temperament Lively and alert.

Head and Skull Head large in comparison to body, rounded but in no way domed, wide between the ears. Hair on skull, in roughs rather coarse. Nose always black, as short as possible with large open nostrils, high set sloping back to skull with deep stop between nose and skull. Wide muzzle, neat lips, with good turn-up. Chin prominent, in roughs furnished with beard.

Eyes Black rimmed, very dark, large, round, clear and alert.

Ears Semi-erect, high-set, the smaller the better.

Mouth Slightly undershot with even teeth, not showing teeth or tongue.

Neck Medium length, slightly arched, springing from well laid back shoulders.

Forequarters Chest rather wide and deep, legs straight of medium length and bone.

Body Short back, level from withers to tail root, neither roaching nor dipping; deep; well-sprung ribs; short, strong loin.

Ch Shenden Viking. Photo: David Paton

Ch Chilka Kelly of Mahnyar

Hindquarters Well muscled thighs of good length, hocks low to ground, turning neither in nor out, stifles well bent.

Feet Small, thick, cat-like with black toenails.

Tail Customarily docked short, carried high, emerging at right angles from level top-line.

Gait/Movement Free with good drive from rear. Moving true coming and going. High stepping front movement undesirable.

Coat
    Roughs: harsh, wiry, free from curl, preferably with undercoat.
    Smooths: short and tight.

Colour Clear red, black or black and rich tan without white markings. In clear red, a darker shade on mask and ears desirable. Ideally each hair should be an even red from tip to root. Frosting on muzzles of mature smooths should not be penalised.

Size From 2.2-4.9kg (5-11lb), most desirable 2.7-4.5kg (6-10lb).

Faults Any departure from the foregoing points should be considered a fault and the seriousness with which the fault should be regarded should be in exact proportion to its degree.

Note Male animals should have two apparently normal testicles fully descended into the scrotum.

Ch Starbeck Lyric Fantasy.

The Griffon Bruxellois Affixes

Early British affixes: 1900 to 1939

AUSTRAL	Mrs Powell
BABBACOMBE	Miss Clay
BARENTHA	Mrs Osbert Eyre
BROOKVILLE	Mrs Shambrook
CAUSEWAY	Mrs Sainsbury
CASTLEHAVEN	The Misses Plunket
CLIFTON WOOD	Mrs Richardson
COPTHORNE	Lady Handley Spicer
DeMONS	Mrs Glendower Croft
D'ECOSSE	Mrs Rollo Stuart
GERRARDS	Mrs E M Thomas
GLENARTNEY	Mrs Whaley
GLENWOOD	Mrs Barwell
HONEYWICK	Miss Sargent
RTON	Mrs Cliff
LALAROOKH	Mrs Bridle
LAVENDERWAY	Mr F Mitchell
MEADOWLANDS	Miss Fyson
NITSUA	Mrs Fletcher Austin
PARTRIDGE HALL	Mrs Parker Rhodes
PARK PLACE	Miss Hall
RUSKINGTON	Mrs Clarke Black
ST MARGARET	Mrs Charters
SHELVEY	Miss A Tyler
SHENDEN	Miss A Baylay★
SKIBBEREEN	Mrs E Street
SUNNYMEAD	Miss A J Johnson
VULCAN	The Hon Mrs Ionides
WILLGORE	Mrs Williams

★ Mrs P Crick took over SHENDEN on Miss A Baylay's death

British Affixes 1939 to 1969

ALLIDALE	Mr H Greenhalgh
ANDAVE	Mrs A Byrne
ANTEES	Mr J W Barker
ARDTIGHE	Mrs Saunders
BARRATELLE	Miss Sautelle Barter
BERLEYGILL	Mr J Fothergill
BILFORD	Mrs D Price
BLACKROOT	Mrs K Wilton
BOWERHINTON	Mrs M Fearfield, MBE
BUKA	Mrs Osborne
BURWARDSLEY	Mr & Mrs K Davis
CAROSSA	Mrs C Savage
CATOBECK	Miss J M Butler
CAVERSHAM	Mrs H Warner Hill

CHILKA	Mrs W Barker
CHOSENDALE	Mr D Gregory
CLEEVEVIEW	Mrs B Rumney
CROSSGATE	Mrs M E Searl
DAJELA	Mr & Mrs Dorward
DOZMARE	Miss M Downie
DREDA	Mrs D Posnett
DUBRAW	Mrs M Wood
DUNDRY	Mrs F Tuckwell
ENAVANT	Miss Forwood
FORSHAW	Miss J Deeley
GAYSTOCK	Miss Tessa Gaines
GERRARDS	Miss E M Thomas
GLENALDA	Mrs A Wolstenholme
GLENRIG	Mr & Mrs Ellithorn
GORSEDENE	Mrs L Davis
GOSMORE	Mrs A Dallison
GREGTOI	The Misses Gregory
GRIFFJOY	Mrs J W Pratt
INCATON	Mrs P Bird
INCHLEE	Mr & Mrs D Connor
JAYDEAN	Mr & Mrs Higgins
JAKESAMDOR	Mrs D Hunkin
JOLENGRA	Mr & Mrs J Shipley
JORIEMOUR	Mrs M Clark
KEITOY	Mr K Langston
KIRKMARLAND	Mrs Ivine Lowther
KRANDON	Mrs P Woolford
LAUROSE	Mr & Mrs Sie
LIAMFORD	Mrs Burr
LINKFIELD	Mrs M Wheeler
LITAHNI	Miss B Gorringe
MAHNYAR	Mrs Raynham
MANMIST	Mr E Hall
MARGIDUNUM	Mrs B Wilde
MARKATH	Mr & Mrs Burke
MARICOATE	Mrs M Holt
McGOOGANS	Mrs C Gillies
MERRYWEATHER	Mrs E Bassett
MOERANGI	Mrs M Grocott
MOLACH	Mrs Stuart
MONOCEROUS	Mr A MacLellan
MOUNTWHISTLE	Mrs N Marshall
MUNJEY	Mrs Rathbone
OPERASTAR	Mr & Mrs A Murray
OTTERBOURNE	Mrs M Dixon
PANACHE	Mrs M D Brookes
POLROSE	Mrs H Cuming
POTTLE	Mrs E Pearse
PRESTBURY	Mrs Rimmer
UATT	Mrs J Cottrell
QUINTAIL	Mrs E Quinnell
RATHENIS	Mr & Mrs M Payne
RAVENVIEW	Mrs E Bunting

REMOSA	Miss I Lovejoy
REMRAF	Mrs E Farmer
RINGROSE	Miss Cawley
ROLLSVUE	Miss E MacDonald
ROSSUT	Mrs C Sutton
ROWELL	Miss P Date
SEAGRY	Miss M Cousins
SHANDAFF	Mrs B Cooke
SHELVEY	Miss A Tyler
SHENDEN	Mrs P Crick★
SHERWAY	Nr & Mrs J Wheeler
SPEEDWELL	Mrs Kirk
STARBECK	Mrs A Fenn
STERNROC	Mrs P Cross-Stern
STOURAVON	Mrs D Harris
STRAZDA	Mrs Story-Liell
STRONDOUR	Mrs Walker
St ERME	Mrs M Cardew
TATNUM	Miss J Irish
THATCHWAY	Mr & Mrs C Bannister
TOYMORE	Mrs O M Lewis
TUMPFA	Mr & Mrs D Davitt
TUNLAKE	Miss R Deck
TZIGANE	Mrs A Proctor
UPYONDER	Mrs Luxton-Jones
UTOPIAN	Mrs H Enders
VADENTORP	Mrs J B Allen
WENDLITT	Mrs H Littmoden & Mrs W Spencer
WYLHYLDA	Mr Popejoy
WYNWORTH	Mrs Winner

★ Mrs P Crick took over SHENDEN on Miss A Baylay's death

British affixes registered since 1969

ALDERLEIGH	Mr & Mrs J B Townsend
APTRICK	Mrs M Sugden
ASTERAN	Miss R Lancaster
BAJALONS	Mrs D Ballard
BEAUVIEW	Mr & Mrs H Ogden
BEMBRIDGE	Mr P Watkins
BERGADIAN	Mrs G Berg
BILCHRY	Mr W Bradbury
BOBENUT	Mrs E Lunn
BOLMACS	Mrs J Warrington
BOSTROM	Mr, Mrs & Miss Hay
CALLSIGN	Mr B Bury
CANNONGATE	Mrs J Kitchener
CARLTON	Mrs Bull
CLEEVECLOUD	Mrs S Hamlett
COPPERMOON	Mrs M Englefield
CYNJON	Mrs C M Howard
DONZEATA	Mr D Guy

DORELOVE	Mr & Mrs N Swan
DUSKGLOW	Miss Robinson
ELI-JISHANOR	Mr & Mrs J Gibson
EMONA	Mrs A Norris
ENCHANTYA	Mrs C Bloor
FENNYMORE	Mr & Mrs P Mercer
FROMEBANK	Mrs S A Pocock
GEMTOR	Mr & Mrs Marshall
GEMMIFERA	Mrs J M Woods
HARJOY	Mrs P Betteridge
HARLAND	Mr & Mrs Wiley
HIYA	Miss M K Williams
IREBRI	Miss M Bricoe
JENICKO	Mrs J Persson
JEROCA	Mr & Mrs Coombesa & Mr Ellicott
JIVIFI	Miss J Ford
KETTLEDEN	Mrs M Reid
KLANSTED	Mr C J Cray
LAREVE	Mr I J Thompson
MANSU	Mrs C McFarlane
MARILENA	Mrs Metcalf
MARQUANT	Mrs A Edwards
MARSHDAE	Mrs A Marshall
MENWINNION	Miss M Marshall
NORREL	Mr & Mrs Trotter
PETREHAWK	Mr & Mrs P Hawkins
POLCOT	Mrs M Day
PUGNUS	Mr E Herold
REILLERG	Mr P Grellier
ROYDWOOD	Mr M Boothroyde
SHIARITA	Mrs L Stannard
SIJASA	Mr & Mrs Burt
SIROSADOR	Mrs D Bentley
STRIENA	Mrs E Poolman
SUPERLION	Mrs Y Gillibrand
TANTORI	Mr A & Miss C Smith
TNEGUN	Mrs E Nugent
TRAGBAND	Mr A Brace
TUTTLEBEES	Mr N E Butcher
VAIRETTE	Mrs E P Bishop
WENJON	Mr & Mrs J Usher
WILICOT	Mr & Mrs R Henny
WILJAYS	Mrs J M Smart
WITCHAVEN	Mrs R Sims
ZUTHIS	Mr & Mrs Roberts

Note

Not all the names on the list of affixes are current breeder/exhibitors, and neither are all the breeders listed since 1969 new to dog breeding. Some have changed or added to their dog breeding programmes to include the Griffon Bruxellois. However, it is of interest for novice Griffon breeders and pet owners alike to check on their own dog's pedigree.

Champions Since 1964

Name	Owner	Breeder
1990-1997 Champions		
Dogs		
Ch Cynjon Bitter Sweet	Mrs C Howard	Owner
Ch Inchlee Fireflash	Mr & Mrs D Connor	Owner
Ch Starbeck Rainboy Quest	Mrs A Fenn	Owner
Ch Starbeck Santa Claus	Mrs A Fenn	Owner
Ch Stewell Golly Gosh	Mr S Bardwell	Owner
Ch Shenden Gershwin	Mrs P Crick	Owner
Ch Fromebank Eastend Lad	Mrs S Pocock	Owner
Ch Marquant He's Rett	Mr & Mrs Price	Owners
Ch Operastar Nutcracker	Mr & Mrs Murray	Owners
Ch Fennymore Spankin' Good Time	Mr & Mrs Mercer	Owners
Bitches		
Ch Fennymore Blazinickers	Mrs M Mercer	Owner
Ch Jaydean First Love	Mrs M Higgins	Owner
Ch Marquant Miss Scarlet	Mrs A Price	Owner
Ch Polcot Touch of Class	Mrs M Day	Owner
Ch Marquant Fallen Angel	Mr & Mrs Price	Owners
Ch Starbeck Moonshell	Mrs A Fenn	Owner

Update on the two Top Dogs:

Ch Dorelove Jimmy Mac now holds the record of 57 CCs.

Ch Starbeck Crystal Rainbow holds the record for Toy Group and BIS awards at Championship Shows.

Name	Owner	Breeder
1984-1990 Champions		
Dogs		
Ch Starbeck Citation	Mrs A Fenn	Owner
Ch Striena Barnaby Rudge	Mrs P Poolman	Owner
Ch Petrehawk Rockafella of Jaydean	Mrs M Higgins	Mr P Hawkins
Ch Operastar Chu Chin Chow	Mrs Murray	Owner
Ch Starbeck Crystal Rainbow	Mrs A Fenn	Owner
Ch Maricoate Jo Jo of Dorelove	Mr & Mrs N Swan	Mrs Holt
Ch Joriemour Thomas	Mrs M Clark	Owner
Ch Fennymore National Elf	Mr & Mrs Mercer	Owners
Ch Bobenut Mr Tod	Mrs E Lunn	Owner
Ch Dorelove Jimmy Mac	Mr & Mrs N Swan	Owners
Ch Joriemour Right As Rain	Mrs M Clark	Owner
Ch Fennymore Playing With Fire	Mr & Mrs Mercer	Owners
Ch Petrehawk Challenger	Mr P Hawkins	Owner
Ch Jaydean Cole Porter	Mrs M Higgins	Owner
Ch Gaystock L'Incroyable	Miss T Gaines	Owner
Bitches		
Ch Dozmare Damask Rose	Miss M Downie	Owner
Ch Speedwell Winsome	Mrs D Kirk	Owner
Ch Starbeck Silken Knot	Mrs A Fenn	Owner
Ch Cleeveview Calypso	Mrs B Rumney	Owner
Ch Ardtighe Quince	Mrs J Saunders	Owner
Ch Dorelove Maggie May	Mr & Mrs N Swan	Owners
Ch Starbeck Circus Flame	Mrs A Fenn	Owner
Ch Winch Lady Rogue	Mr P Hawkins	Mmes Crawford & Thomas
Ch Starbeck Calendula	Mrs A Fenn	Owner

Name	Owner	Breeder
Ch Fennymore My Dad's Cute	Mr & Mrs Mercer	Owners
Ch Litahni Witch	Miss B Gorringe	Owner
Ch Starbeck Crown Treasure	Mrs A Fenn	Owner
Ch Starbeck Crinoline	Mrs A Fenn	Owner
Ch Mahnyar Dragonfly	Mrs D Raynham	Owner
Ch Fennymore Jolly Hocki Stix	Mr & Mrs Mercer	Owners
Ch Gaystock Gold Medaille	Miss T Gaines	Owner
Ch Cynjon Glamour Girl	Mr & Mrs Howard	Owners
Ch Starbeck Crystal Song	Mrs A Fenn	Owner
Ch Harland Ratiffany	Mrs N Wiley	Owner
Ch Starbeck Crystal Tang	Mrs A Fenn	Owner
Ch Shiarita The Naughty Pixie	Mr & Mrs Stannard	Owners
Ch Fennymore Code Name Gertie	Mr & Mrs Mercer	Owners
Ch Operastar Casta Diva	Mr & Mrs Murray	Owners
Ch Fennymore Runonbatteries	Mr & Mrs Mercer	Owners

1980-1983 Champions

Dogs

Name	Owner	Breeder
Ch Litahni Coppernob	Miss B Gorringe	Owner
Ch Operastar Jack Point	Mrs B Murray	Owner
Ch Joriemour Pinnochio	Mrs M Clark	Owner
Ch Shenden Gamblers Dream	Mrs P Crick	Owner
Ch Starbeck Chinrullah	Mrs A Fenn	Owner
Ch Markath Harbour Light	Mr & Mrs K Burke	Owners
Ch Gaystock Tour de Force	Mrs & Miss Gaines	Owners
Ch Beauview Bona Fide	Mr H Ogden	Owner
Ch Starbeck Chindit	Mrs A Fenn	Owner
Ch Mountwhistle Bees Knees	Mrs N Marshall	Owner

Name	Owner	Breeder
Ch Maricoate Tom Tom of Dorelove	Mr & Mrs N Swan	Mr M Holt
Ch Keidrey Copper Dancer	Mr & Mrs Guest	Mr & Mrs Norman

Bitches

Ch Andiron Miss Muppet	Mrs P Wiggins	Owner
Ch Mahnyar Tiptoes	Mrs D Raynham	Owner
Ch Burwardsley Royal Lady	Mrs A Edwards	Mrs Davis
Ch Mountwhistle Charm	Mrs N Marshall	Owner
Ch Starbeck Calinks	Mrs A Fenn	Owner
Ch Operastar Mignon	Mrs B Murray	Owner
Ch Ardtighe Nerine of Kettledean	Mrs M Reid	Mrs Saunders
Ch Cleeveview Satin	Mrs E Lunn	Mrs B Rumney
Ch Operastar Fledermaus	Mrs B Murray	Owner
Ch Pottle Black Petal	Mr E Hall	Mrs Pearce
Ch Jaydean By George	Mrs M Higgins	Owner

Champions 1973-1979

Dogs

Ch Ardtighe Edouard	Mrs Saunders	Owner
Ch Barretelle The Artist	Miss Sautelle Barter	Owner
Ch Burwardsley Grasshopper	Mrs H Day	Mrs Davis
Ch Chilka Kelly of Mahnyar	Mrs D Raynham	Mrs Barker
Ch Chosendale Seamus	Mrs Dangerfield	Mr D Gregory
Ch Chosendale Crispin	Mr D Gregory	Miss D MacDonald
Ch Gerrards New Penny	Miss E Gorringe	Miss E Thomas
Ch Winter's Melody of Gregtoi	The Misses Gregory	Owners
Ch Krandon Jumbo Jet	Mrs P Woolford	Owner
Ch Krandon Storm Warning	Mrs Warrington	Mrs P Woolford

Name	Owner	Breeder
Ch Markath Harbour Light	Mrs Burke	Owner
Ch Otterbourne Ojomo	Mr & Mrs J Dixon	Owners
Ch Otterbourne Olysnuff	Mr & Mrs J Dixon	Owners
Ch Remosa Relko of Otterbourne	Mrs M Dixon	Miss I Lovejoy
Ch Skibbereen Shandaff Danield	Mrs E Street	Mrs B Cooke
Ch Skibbereen Black Magic	Mrs P Bird	Mrs E Street
Ch Skibbereen Golden Shade	Mrs E Street	Owner
Ch Speedwell Gambol	Mrs D Kirk	Owner
Ch Speedwell Quest	Mrs D Kirk	Owner
Ch Starbeck Cristominsky	Mrs A Fenn	Owner
Ch Starbeck Fusilier	Mrs Dix	Mrs A Fenn

Bitches

Name	Owner	Breeder
Ch Allidale Francesca	Mr Greenhalgh	Owner
Ch Andiron Charley Girl	Mrs P Wiggins	Owner
Ch Burwardsley Emma	Mrs M Higgins	Mrs Davis
Ch Chilka Holly of Mahnyar	Mrs D Raynham	Mrs Barker
Ch Chosendale Nutmeg	Mr D Gregory	Owner
Ch Dozmare Damsel	Miss M Downie	Owner
Ch Dubraw Dubouche	Mrs M Wood	Owner
Ch Dubraw Simone	Miss U Gregory	Mrs M Wood
Ch Gerrards Red Rose	Miss E Thomas	Owner
Ch Golden Allegretto of Glenrig	Mr & Mrs Ellithorn	Owners
Ch Golden Symbol of Glenrig	Mr & Mrs Ellithorn	Owners
Ch Petal of Gregtoi	The Misses Gregory	The Misses Gregory
Ch Concorde of Krandon	Mrs P Woolford	Owner
Ch Mountwhistle Rosanova	Mrs Marshall	Owner
Ch Mahnyar Tiller Girl	Mrs D Raynham	Owner

Name	Owner	Breeder
Ch Operastar Phoebe	Mrs A Murray	Owner
Ch Rathenis Puss in Boots	Mrs P Wiggins	Mr & Mrs M Payne
Ch Shenden Gwyneth	Mrs P Crick	Miss A Baylay
Ch Shenden Gypsy Melody	Mrs P Crick	Miss A Baylay
Ch Skibbereen Pierrette	Mrs E Street	Owner
Ch Speedwell Katrina	Mrs D Kirk	Owner
Ch Speedwell Suzy	Mrs D Kirk	Owner
Ch Starbeck Cristaminta	Mrs A Fenn	Owner
Ch Starbeck Cristanella	Mrs A Fenn	Owner
Ch Starbeck Chirimoya	Mrs A Fenn	Owner
Ch Starbeck Columbine	Mrs A Fenn	Owner
Ch Starbeck Cristabelle	Mrs A Fenn	Owner
Ch Starbeck Chingle Bell	Mrs A Fenn	Owner
Ch Sternroc Marmalade Sundae	Mr & Mrs M Dixon	Mrs P Cross-Stern
Ch Strondour Secks a Peel	Mrs Reid	Mrs M Walker

Champions 1968-1972

Dogs

Name	Owner	Breeder
Ch Shendon Garrison	Miss A Baylay	Owner
Ch Keitoy Kismet	Mr K Langston	Owner
Ch Primus Molach	Miss J Stuart	Owner
Ch Gaystock le Nouveau	Mrs D Gaines	Owner
Ch Gaystock Monsieur le Maire	Mrs D Gaines	Owner
Ch Rossut Tintomo of Caversham	Mrs C Sutton	Mrs Palmer
Ch Dozmare Sprite	Mrs B Wild	Mrs M Downie
Ch Starbeck Fireking	Mrs A Fenn	Owner

Name	Owner	Breeder
Ch Hunters Melody of Gregtoi	Mr H Ogden	The Misses Gregory
Ch Sternroc Marmalade Minstral	Mrs P Cross-Stern	Owner
Ch Bowerhinton Coco of Linkfield	Mrs M Fearfield,	Miss M Wheeler
Ch Skibbereen Golden Shade	Mrs E Street	Owner
Bitches		
Ch Skibbereen Joriemour Fabiola	Mrs E Street	Mrs M Clark
Ch Skibbereen Brabjoy Estralita	Mrs E Street	Mr & Mrs Lane
Ch Enavant Psyche	Miss M Forwood	Owner
Ch Rathenis Miss Wet Feet	Mr & Mrs M Payne	Owners
Ch Joriemour Victoria	Mrs M Clark	Owner
Ch Skibbereen Panache Mona Lisa	Mrs E Street	Mrs M Brookes
Ch Shenden Gaystock la Boheme	Miss A Baylay	Mrs D Gaines
Ch Skibbereen Lalita	Mrs E Street	Mrs Chapman Smith
Ch Chosendale Louella	Mrs B Rumney	Mr D Gregory
Ch Golden Harmony of Glenrig	Mr & Mrs Ellithorn	Owners
Ch Skibbereen Juliana	Mrs E Street	Owner
Ch Dozmare Della	Miss M Downie	Owner
Ch Starbeck Cristina	Mrs A Fenn	Owner
Ch Barratelle Anitra's Song	Miss Sautelle Barter	Owner
Ch Osaka of Otterbourne	Mrs M Dixon	Owner
Ch Chosendale Munjey Pollyanna	Mr D Gregory	Mrs P Rathbone
Ch Shenden Gwyneth	Mrs P Crick	Miss A Baylay

Champions 1964-1968

Dogs

Ch Thatchway Cruiser	Mr & Mrs C Bannister	Owners
Ch Bowerhinton Billy Bee	Mrs M Fearfield	Owner

Name	Owner	Breeder
Ch Brutus of Margidumum	Mrs B Wilde	Mrs King
Ch Ruskington Remy	Mrs D Kirk	Mrs Clarke Black
Ch Enavant Golden Baronet	Mrs M Forwood	Miss Sautelle Barter
Ch Enavant Barbican	Miss M Forwood	Owner
Ch Gay Cavalier of Kirkmarland	Mr Irving-Lowther	Owner
Ch Black Arrow of Gregtoi	The Misses Gregory	Owners
Ch Skibbereen Oliver of Otterbourne	Mrs E Street	Mrs M Dixon
Ch Oscar of Otterbourne	Mrs M Dixon	Owner
Ch Bowerhinton Billy Simon	Mrs G Sehlstedt	Mrs M Fearfield
Ch Golden Hind of Gregtoi	M Belli	The Misses Gregory
Ch Barratelle Red Robin	Miss Sautelle Barter	Owner

Bitches

Name	Owner	Breeder
Ch Joriemour Alexandra	Mrs M Clark	Owner
Ch Skibbereen Alexandra	Mrs E Street	Owner
Ch Chosendale Pennicandy of Tunlake	Mr D Gregory	Miss M Deck
Ch Joriemour Margaret	Mrs M Clark	Owner
Ch Annabelle of Kirkmarland	Mr R Irving-Lowther	Owner
Ch Keitoi Kiwi	Mr K Langston	Owner
Ch Victoria Molach	Miss J Stuart	Owner
Ch Glenalda Gi Gi	Mrs A Wolstenholme	Owner
Ch Olive of Otterbourne	Mrs J Pratt	Mrs M Dixon
Ch Antees Amoretta	Mr J Barker	Owner
Ch Star Charmer of Gregtoi	Mrs R Taylor	The Misses Gregory

Useful Addresses

Breed Club Secretaries

The Griffon Bruxellois Club
Secretary: Mrs Maria Oliver
20 The Bridle Way
Purley
Surrey CR8 3JA   Tel: 0181 660 0969

The Northern Griffon Bruxellois Club
Secretary: Mrs B Roberts
57 Seymour Street
Birkenhead
Merseyside   L42 5LR   Tel: 0151 647 8748

The Scottish Griffon Bruxellois Club
Secretary: Mrs C Marshall
Gemtor
14 Forres Avenue
Dundee   DD3 0EJ   Tel: 01382 814987

The Griffon Bruxellois Breeders Association
Secretary: Mr Peter Watkins
21C Knox Crescent
Nuneaton
Warwickshire   CV11 6DS   Tel: 01203 346684

Publications

The Griffon Bruxellois Club Bulletin
Editor: Mrs Maria Oliver
20 The Bridle Way
Purley
Surrey   CR8 3JA   Tel: 01233 623812

The Northern Griffon Bruxellois Club Newsletter
Editor: Mrs Maureen Higgins
16 Redhill Avenue
Glasshoughton
Castleford
West Yorkshire WF10 4QH

Progress
The Griffon Bruxellois Breeders Association
Editor: Mrs P M Crick
Westcott House
Napton-on-the Hill
Nr Rugby
Warwickshire   CV23 8NG

Our Dogs
5 Oxford Road
Station Approach
Manchester   M60 1SX

Dog World
9 Tufton Street
Ashford
Kent   TN23 1QN

Miscellaneous

Requirements for Export
Ministry of Agriculture Fisheries and Food
Hook Rise South
Tolworth
Surbiton
Surrey

The Council of Docked Breeds (CDB)
Secretary: Ginette Elliott   *or*   Anne Moore
Marsburg Kennels   Sprogmore Kennels
Whitehall Lane   Main Road
Thorpe-le-Soken   Alresford
Essex   CO10 0AF   Colchester Essex   CO7 8AP

Index

... and finally

We must all be truly grateful to Doone Raynham for taking on the massive task of gathering together all the material for a book about the Griffon Bruxellois. When I asked her why she was doing it, she simply replied,

'Because so many people asked me where they could get a Griffon book full of information about our breed, and I felt so sad to tell them there wasn't one.'

So, encouraged by myself as well as many others, she took on the task, and it has turned out to be full of information. History, breed clubs, showing, breeding, ailments and champions to name just some topics, all illustrated with many photographs. I'm sure that everyone in the breed who reads this book will be so grateful to her for taking it on. Thank you, Doone.

Pat Crick (Shenden)